W9-AUY-203

SAPPHIRES
from Psalms

Books by Linda Newton
Available from Warner Press

12 Ways to Turn Your Pain into Praise

Better Than Jewels

Sapphires from Psalms

SAPPHIRES
from Psalms

31 Days of Biblical Insight for a Woman Seeking God

Linda Newton

Anderson, Indiana

Copyright © 2010 by Linda Newton. All rights reserved. No part of this publication may be reproduced, stored in a retrieval system, or transmitted in any form or by any means—electronic, mechanical, photocopy, recording or any other—except for brief quotations in printed reviews, without prior written permission of the publisher. For this and all other editorial matters, please contact:

Coordinator of Publishing & Creative Services
Church of God Ministries, Inc.
PO Box 2420, Anderson, IN 46018-2420
800-848-2464 • www.chog.org

To purchase additional copies of this book, to inquire about distribution, and for all other sales-related matters, please contact:

Warner Press, Inc.
PO Box 2499, Anderson, IN 46018-2499
800-741-7721 • www.warnerpress.org

All Scripture quotations, unless otherwise indicated, are taken from the Holy Bible, New International Version®. NIV®. Copyright © 1973, 1978, 1984 by International Bible Society. Used by permission of Zondervan. All rights reserved.

Scripture quotations marked NRSV are taken from New Revised Standard Version Bible, copyright 1989, Division of Christian Education of the National Council of the Churches of Christ in the United States of America. Used by permission. All rights reserved.

Scripture quotations marked KJV are taken from the Holy Bible, King James Version.

Scripture quotations marked NLT are taken from the Holy Bible, New Living Translation, copyright © 1996. Used by permission of Tyndale House Publishers, Inc., Wheaton, Illinois 60189. All rights reserved.

Scripture quotations marked MSG are taken from *The Message* by Eugene H. Peterson, copyright (c) 1993, 1994, 1995, 1996, 2000, 2001, 2002. Used by permission of NavPress Publishing Group. All rights reserved.

Cover and text design by Carolyn Frost and Mary Jaracz.
Edited by Joseph D. Allison and Stephen R. Lewis.

ISBN-13: 978-1-59317-511-5

Library of Congress Cataloging-in-Publication Data
Newton, Linda, 1954-
    Sapphires from Psalms : 31 gems of comfort for a woman seeking God / Linda Newton.
        p.   cm.
    ISBN 978-1-59317-511-5 (hardcover)
    1. Bible. O.T. Psalms--Meditations. 2. Christian women--Religious life.
        I. Title.
    BS1430.54.N49 2010
    242'.643--dc22   2010006303

Day 1: Examples

Blessed is the man
    who does not walk in the counsel of the wicked
or stand in the way of sinners
    or sit in the seat of mockers.
But his delight is in the law of the LORD,
    and on his law he meditates day and night.
He is like a tree planted by streams of water,
    which yields its fruit in season
and whose leaf does not wither.
    Whatever he does prospers. (Psalm 1:1–3)

....

Scripture Insight: For years when I read this verse, I saw it as a warning not to listen to the counsel of wicked people, not to *stand* on the path that sinners choose, nor *sit* with the foolish mockers. But as I was reading it one day, the phrase "stand in the way of sinners" struck me in a different way. There are so many things we do that "stand in the way of [i.e., hinder] sinners" from finding the Lord. Judgmental remarks, contentious complaints, lousy attitudes, unrestrained hypocrisy are just a few of our flaws that keep people from embracing God.

As believers, we are the only Bible people read until they read the Bible that they need! With that in mind, I'm learning every day to ask the Lord to empower me with the Holy Spirit, so I can make him look good to a world who desperately needs his love.

Jack and Jillian

Jack and Jillian were the dimpled darlings of their company. It didn't hurt that they had singsong names that sounded like a nursery rhyme. Their clients and co-workers loved them, and for good reason. They were an attractive, kind, and capable couple. In the cutthroat market of the seventies, it was hard to find real estate agents who were fair and honest. These two were because they believed they worked for God.

When the other guys engaged in banter that was less than respectful toward women, Jack declined to participate. When Frannie, the office gossip, started dishing the latest dirt on the other employees or clients, Jillian would subtly shift the topic of conversation until the women were talking civilly again. There was no lecturing or finger pointing, just clever redirection.

This winning couple didn't pepper their conversations with *shoulds* and *oughts*. No narrow judgmental attitude here, just a lot of love and acceptance. They didn't complain about the boss or criticize those around them, and you could always find them at the top if the sales leader board because they brought that same conscientious kindness into their sales calls.

At one lavish company party with an open bar, Jack made his way to the bartender and asked for a Roy Rogers. "That's Coke with grenadine, right?" the bartender had to ask.

"That's right," Jack responded.

"I don't get much call for those kid drinks at shindigs like this when people can get all the booze they want for free. Hope that pomegranate juice isn't to much for ya!" the bartender added sarcastically.

"Coke and pomegranate juice is just my speed," Jack smiled.

An hour passed and Jillian made her way over to the bar. "I'll have a Shirley Temple, please." To her surprise, the bartender doubled over with laughter.

After taking a minute to regain his composure, he said, "You're not going to believe this. I just had some guy come through here and order a Roy Rogers!"

"I know," Jillian replied. "I'm Roy's wife!" The bartender burst into uproarious laughter again.

Jack and Jillian proved they could be in the world but not of the world. Their behavior didn't "stand in the way of sinners." Their actions drew people to the Christ they loved. It was no wonder that when the company secretary was going through a life crisis, she turned to this winsome couple. Over burgers and potato salad, they read verses from Romans and led her to a saving knowledge of Jesus Christ.

While Jack and Jillian led the office in sales—prospering by the world's standards—they believed their greatest achievement was bringing hope to a hurting world by pointing people to God.

Polish Your Jewels:

- What behaviors can you embrace to be more Christlike in the workplace?

- Henry Drummond remarked, "How many prodigals are kept out of the kingdom of God by the unlovely characters of those who profess to be inside!" What behaviors hinder your witness and should be discarded?

- Ask God for the strength to do both.

Day 2: Favor

For surely, O LORD, you bless the righteous;
> you surround them with your favor as with a
> shield. (Psalm 5:12)

....

Scripture Insight: For years I have heard church folks tell stories about parking spaces that instantly came available when they were at the hospital or money that just showed up in the mail. In the early days of my Christian faith, I dismissed those as coincidences misrepresented by overly enthusiastic believers. But the evidence of God's intervention has been too overwhelming for me to discount over the years. I am a firm believer that the things that matter to us matter to God—even the little things.

Rita's Ring

"Your ring is exquisite," I commented to Rita as we stood in line at the church potluck. "I've never seen one like it. Did you have it made for you?"

"Thank you. I love it too" she quickly responded. "Craig had it made for me. It has special meaning."

"The cross in the center is inlaid with opal. Is that your birthstone?"

"It's Craig's and mine. He gave it to me on our seventeenth anniversary, not long after he gave his heart to the Lord. He wasn't always the wonderful guy you see in service on Sundays. For a while there in our marriage, Craig was a real mess.

"When we first got married, we were so close," Rita continued. "But he dove more and more into work, neglecting me and the kids. Before I knew it, we weren't spending any time together, and he was in the arms of a woman at work. It was devastating.

"The weekend before he was ready to move out, his brother convinced him to go to a Promise Keepers meeting. God got a hold of my husband and turned him every way but loose!" Rita's eyes danced at this part of the story. "He broke off his relationship with the woman at work. I even heard his side of a phone conversation telling her not to call him anymore because he wanted to make his marriage work. Then he requested a transfer so he wouldn't have to see her at the office.

"Craig started coming to church with us and spending more time with the family. He went to men's meetings and Bible studies every time the doors were open. On our anniversary, he presented me with this ring. He made a speech when he gave it to me, which is totally not his style, and that made it even more special. He told me that the opal represented the two of us with our lives turned toward the cross, and it was his commitment to stay that way. This ring was my promise that he would keep seeking Christ in our marriage."

"What an awesome story!" I said. "This *is* a special ring."

"Yeah. That's why I was so devastated when I looked down at my hand and my ring was gone. It was the first week I worked in the cafeteria at the kids' school, and I panicked. I had kids combing the floor, but there was no sign of it. I knew I had it on when I washed my hands, just before I went into the cafeteria. It had to be somewhere near there. I asked the cafeteria ladies to keep an eye out, but I didn't hold out a lot of hope. The school has twelve hundred students who all eat in the cafeteria, and ten custodians who work odd hours. In a way, I felt it was shallow to be praying for a ring; but with all Craig and I had been through, I just couldn't lose my precious gift. It meant too much to me. So I breathed a prayer for the Lord to bring it back to me."

Now I was hooked on Rita's story. I had to know what happened. We were through the potluck line and sitting at the table with our plates.

"A week to the day later, I was going to work in my daughter's classroom," Rita continued, "so I went by the cafeteria. I asked one of the ladies behind the counter if she had any news of my ring. As she was shaking her head no, a man in a custodian's uniform spoke up.

"I had never seen the guy before. He walked over and asked, 'Could this be the ring you're talking about?' He pulled my ring out of his pocket and said, 'I was sweeping up last night and there it was.'

"I think I screamed when I saw it. 'It's been a week since I lost it,' I told him. 'This is unbelievable! There have been several hundred people in here since I lost this tiny thing.'"

"'Yeah,' he said. 'I'm not usually here for the day shift, but I just started night school, so they let me come in and work today.'"

I shook my head in amazement.

"Linda, God truly did bring my ring back to me. The fact that this man found it a week after it was gone and he just *happened* to be sitting in the cafeteria when I just *happened* to be asking about my ring. It was clearly a 'God thing'!"

"Or a God ring," I offered. We both laughed and marveled about God's painstaking care.

Polish Your Jewels

- Do you believe that God cares about even the little things in your life?

- Test him on this and watch how he proves he is faithful.

- Does knowing that he cares about the things you care about—no matter how small—further confirm his unquenchable love for you?

- Take time to thank him for his painstaking care.

Day 3: Joyful Noise

I will give thanks to the LORD because of
          his righteousness
     and will sing praise to the name of the
          LORD Most High. (Psalm 7:17)

....

Scripture Insight: I always wished I had a talent for singing. After trying hard for years to be a musical person, I gave up and decided to marry one. I've made peace with the fact that God gave me gifts that did not include being a member of the worship team.

Soothing Sound?

I play the radio; that's the extent of my musical skills. It wasn't for lack of trying. I played in the band for years in high school and tried choir in college, but all that did was demonstrate my lack of musical talent. So with each of my pregnancies I selfishly asked God to bless my babies with their daddy's gift of music.

My husband Bruce can sing and play a variety of musical instruments. To my great delight, God answered my prayers and all three of my children are musically gifted. While my daughters can sing like birds, it is my son Jake who followed in his dad's footsteps and learned to play instruments. He would trail around behind his dad, imitating guitar licks.

He moved on to master the mandolin, banjo, and some keyboard riffs. He and his sisters learned to harmonize when their dad could get them to sit still long enough. Jake invested so much in his music that he ended up attending college on a music scholarship.

I should not have been surprised by Jake's response when he was a baby. As I sat rocking and singing to my precious tow-headed bundle, his fat little hand came up and grabbed my chin, his pudgy fingers wrapped around my bottom teeth. With a pained expression on his face, he pleaded, "Mommy no sing. Daddy sing. *Mommy no sing.*"

Considering the talent that became apparent later, it must have been sheer torture for the poor child to listen to his mother's pitiful pitch and tone! When I sing praises to the Lord now, I do it under my breath. And I thank God that he cares more about my heart than my harmony.

Polish Your Jewels

- Have you ever wished you had gifts that weren't yours?

- Take inventory of all gifts God *has* given you.

- Nurture those gifts. Praise him for what you have instead of pining for what you don't.

Day 4: Grace

When I look at your heavens, the work of your fingers,
    the moon and the stars that you have established;
what are human beings that you are mindful of them,
    mortals that you care for them?
Yet you have made them a little lower than God,
    and crowned them with glory and honor.

(Psalm 8:3-5 NRSV)

Scripture Insight: When I read majestic scriptures like this one, I marvel at how a holy God can care so much for a human being as flawed as I. And I am grateful that he does. God is so much more than "mindful" of us. His grace is endless and his love for us—even in our stubborn sinfulness—is unmistakable.

From Tough Guy to Tender Heart

I opened my mailbox one day and found a note addressed to my husband and me from Kenny, a seasonal firefighter in our church. Kenny's letters were consistent, supportive, and always timely. This one was no exception. It read:

Dear Bruce and Linda,

I hope and continue to pray that all is going well back home. The crew and I are still on the five-thousand-acre Big Meadow Fire in Yosemite National Park. I was thinking today about how awesome your job is. It's not really a job but a beautiful gift from God. I know it might not seem that way sometimes, but a ministry that takes care of the spiritual needs of people all the time, and the blessings that come with that, has got to be the next best thing to heaven.

God has put such high value on us. Psalm 8:4–5 says, "What is man that you are mindful of him, the son of man that you care for him. You have made him a little lower than the heavenly beings and crowned him with glory and honor."

Bruce and Linda, as pastors of our church, you acknowledge that value endlessly by living out the gift that God has given you. How awesome!

Thanks for doing that and for being so kind and supportive for my daughters all of these years. With all you had going on, you still took time to encourage, comfort, and guide them when I was away on fires. I can never repay your kindness.

Keep up the good non-work. Your relentless effort is priceless, and your blessings will be continuous all the way into heaven!

God's love and mine,

Ken

Kenny's positive note affirmed his statement. We have saved a drawer full of his wonderful notes. What an encourager! As I thought about our firefighting friend, I realized how far God has brought him.

Like many parents, Kenny followed his kids to church. He was newly divorced with custody of his three young daughters. Kenny was a tough trapper whose greatest thrill was to sleep on the ground for days on end and hunt animals for their fur. The job of fighting fires in national forests was tailor-made for this wild man. Since the divorce, he had begun drinking heavily and had survived more than a few barroom brawls. He was bad and getting worse, until God stepped in.

A neighbor named Paula thought Kenny's beautiful daughters could use some feminine influence, so she invited the girls to church. When they started to attend our services every week, he decided he needed "to check out those holy-rollers."

The day Kenny drove the girls to church, the parking lot was full. We needed a new building that could hold everyone who called Sierra Pines their church home, but until that happened, finding room—especially in the parking lot—was a problem.

My husband Bruce was usually busy on Sunday mornings between our two worship services, meeting and greeting people, as well as prepping for his next sermon. However, Bruce *just happened* to be walking across the parking lot when Kenny and the girls pulled in. Seeing how crowded it was, the tough guy began to drive away when Bruce stepped in front of his truck. He motioned for Kenny to park his pick-up under a tree, the only spot left anywhere on the grounds.

To Kenny's surprise, the man who found a parking place for him was the same guy who stood up to preach that day. He sat through the service with a scowl, but he had to admit he really liked it. He heard Bruce talk about God's love and grace, without the blame and judgmentalism Kenny had expected.

Kenny continued to come with his girls. The folks in church wrapped their arms around him, despite his skeptical scowl. The sermons gave him hope for a better life, and after three weeks he even let a smile slip across his face during one of those sermons.

God loved this wild man and went to great lengths to prove it. Kenny hadn't been at church more than a few weeks when he got called out on a dangerous fire. This was the kind of assignment he lived for. After many weary days with thousands of acres burning all around, Kenny told his crew to fall back while he climbed out onto a ledge to assess the fire and determine their next move. At that moment, the wind shifted and the fire turned on him.

Instinctively, Kenny deployed his fire shelter. Every firefighter was equipped with a thin "pup tent" made of fiberglass and aluminum that could withstand heat up to 500 degrees before it began to delaminate. It was to be used as a last resort if a man was trapped by fire. Kenny struggled to hold the shelter over himself as the wind howled and toxic fumes blew through the tent. The heat was unbearable. His shelter began breaking apart. He could feel the searing heat as the fire burned over him, making it nearly impossible to keep his shelter in place. In that moment, Kenny heard God say, "I'm not finished with you yet."

He felt himself losing consciousness, but knew that he couldn't hold down the shelter in that event. So he prayed, "Lord, I leave my life in your hands. Take care of my children."

At that moment, the wind let up, the pitch black darkness turned to light, and he got a breath of cooler air. When he reached the end of his own strength, he let God take over. He knew then he was going to be all right.

"Since God spared my life, I decided to give it all to him. I wasn't doing such a great job of things without him anyway," Kenny confessed as he told me this story several weeks later. "I'm so grateful for his grace that I want to give back to him in every way I can."

Kenny has lived up to those words. He is a faithful volunteer leader for both junior-high and senior-high youth groups. He gives generously to his church and additionally to special projects. This forgiven follower also sends volumes of letters of encouragement to his Christian family members everywhere.

Ken's daughters are also delightful examples of God's love. They have all gone on mission trips in all kinds of cultures. His middle daughter, Jodi, now works as the church's children's ministry coordinator. God even blessed this tough guy with a new wife who is also a seasoned firefighter and understands the struggles of his life on the fire line because she has lived them.

This one-time skeptic may marvel at the psalmist's comment, "What is man that you are mindful of him?" but I think God has made a good investment in Kenny's life!

Polish Your Jewels

- Is there a person in your neighborhood like Kenny, who seems unlikely to become a citizen of God's kingdom? Ask God to give you love for that person and his/her family.

- Pray for that neighbor every day. Ask God to soften that person's heart.

- Pray for the courage to invite your neighbor to church. Then do it.

Day 5: Livelihood

The LORD is a refuge for the oppressed
    a stronghold in times of trouble.
Those who know your name will trust in you,
    for you, LORD, have never forsaken those who
    seek you. (Psalm 9:9–10)

....

Scripture Insight: There are times when we can't imagine
with our limited perspective how God is going to resolve
our problems. We have to remind ourselves that his
perspective is not limited, neither are his resources. When
intimidating situations appear, we can trust God to take us
through them. We need to make prayer our first response,
not our last resort. That's what Nancy did.

Nancy's New Job

Nancy was born to work with babies. I never saw a
child she couldn't calm or a mother who didn't feel
utter confidence leaving her baby in Nancy's care.

"Nancy, what you have is a calling, not just a job," I told
her one Sunday as we sat together in the church nursery.

"I'm blessed," she responded. "I love these kids like they
are my own."

The church staff felt so fortunate to have Nancy as our
nursery director, and clearly Nancy felt led to be there.

Not long after we had this conversation, I got an early morning call at the church from Nancy. "Linda, I need your prayers," she said.

"You've got them. What's going on?"

"My boss just called me and said I have to start working on Sundays. I explained that I already have a job working at the church, and I even told him about two other people on the payroll who wanted to work those hours, but he stubbornly refused to hear anything I had to say."

"Did you tell him that it's a paying job, not just a volunteer position?" I asked. Perhaps her boss would respect the fact that she had employment elsewhere that day.

"I did, but he didn't seem to care. Linda, I love my job with the kids during the first service, and I need to go to worship to 'fill my tank' during the second. I would quit my job at the hardware store, but I need the money. I don't know how God is going to pull this out. Will you pray for me to have faith?"

"You got it," I said. "Let's pray right now, and I'll keep praying until you get an answer."

I began, "Lord, we know that nothing surprises you. You knew before time began everything that Nancy would need. Father, I believe you are the one who gifted her with the skill and desire to work with babies, and I believe you have called her to that ministry. I am asking you to make a way for her to do that. You have a job already picked out for her that will take care of her financial needs, so I pray that you will give her the strength to wait on you and trust you to show her what that is. Amen."

"Thank you," Nancy sniffed.

"I'm still praying. Feel my prayers carry you through the day."

As I walked through the door from work that day, my husband told me Nancy had called. "She wants you to call her back right away."

I could hear the excitement in Nancy's voice when she answered the phone. "Linda, you're not going to believe this. Just after I talked with you this morning, I went to run some errands. I stopped to get gas and saw my friend Susan, whom I hadn't seen in five years. We were catching up, and before I could even tell her about my situation, she blurted out, 'Do you need a job? I've got one for you.' We used to work at the same place and we worked well together."

Susan drove a bus in town for developmentally disabled people. It was a 9-to-5 job with weekends off. One of their drivers had just quit and the job hadn't even been posted yet.

"Here," Susan said, handing Nancy a card. "Call this lady and tell her we talked. Tell her I'm your reference."

"Linda, Susan's boss hired me on the spot! And the job even has benefits!" Nancy exclaimed.

"When I called my boss at the hardware store to give him my two weeks' notice, he told me I didn't even have to come in, so I won't miss a single Sunday. God is so good."

"This couldn't happen to a nicer person. I'm thrilled for you, and for the kids at church too!"

"This time it's my turn to pray," Nancy insisted. We prayed together over the phone and thanked God for his amazing answer—within hours of when we first asked.

Polish Your Jewels

- The Psalms often show us how to turn trials into triumphs. See how David's *frustration* (Psalm 13:1–2) that he can't hear from God moves him to *examination* (Psalm 32:5). That results in *realization* (Psalm 32:8–11) that God is in control and a *determination*, (Psalm 55:22) to let him be. All of this leads to a *transformation* (Psalm 126:3-6) toward trust in God.

- Write out this sequence and stick it in your Bible. Make it a bookmark in the Psalms and read it when your faith is challenged.

Day 6: Envy

LORD, you have assigned me my portion and my cup;
    you have made my lot secure.
The boundary lines have fallen for me in pleasant
    places;
    surely I have a delightful inheritance.

(Psalm 16:5–6)

....

Scripture Insight: Nothing robs my joy quicker than comparing myself to other people. It makes it impossible to relish the present because I feel like I'm not measuring up. It keeps me from trying in the future because I feel, "What's the use? I'll be outdone anyway." Comparing causes me to pine away about the past with a long list of, "Woulda, coulda, shouldas." Then I am rendered useless for God today.

This verse helps me to realize that my lot is secure and the boundary lines of my life have fallen for me in pleasant places. Now when I am tempted to compare, I now review those boundary lines. I write out a list of my blessings and read it once a day, especially when I find I'm comparing myself to someone else. This moves me from paralysis to productivity as I recognize that I truly do have a delightful inheritance.

A Healthy Portion

Natalie was a real go-getter. She made it a point to excel at whatever she did. She didn't feel like she had a choice. Growing up with an angry alcoholic father and a mother who blamed her every time dad got mad, Natalie learned to be perfect. "If there was a chance that I would get any approval or love in my home, I had to dot every *I* and cross every *T*. It was exhausting," she admitted, "but the alternative was dad's drunken rage and mom's angry rejection."

When we met for counseling, Natalie demonstrated the same high standards of achievement as she did everywhere else. She was a quick study and made progress in many areas except when it came to comparing herself to others. Despite the fact that such thinking caused her to circle the drain in despair, she couldn't seem to stop herself.

Because dad drank away money for her college education, Natalie applied for junior college and entered the work force. She excelled at both, but earning a living on her own demanded that she work more. Working more meant she had to cut back on her classes.

"I work so much harder than the girls in my office. They show up late and take long lunches to shop. Then I'm the one who gets passed over for promotions because I don't have a college degree. It just doesn't seem fair.

"My boss has no heart. She has no idea what it's like in the real world. She went to college on a trust fund her grandmother set up for her, and she could devote herself to studying because she didn't have to work. Now she has a husband who buys her anything she wants so she doesn't need all the money the company pays her," she lamented in an honest moment as she dumped some of her frustration.

"Maybe she has no heart because she hasn't had to suffer," I offered.

"I agree with you that it doesn't seem fair, but to move forward we have to focus on what we have, not what we don't have. We have to see what's in our cup, not what's not. What do you have going for you right now?"

Natalie reluctantly began to list a few things. As she continued, I watched her countenance change.

"I love my classes. While I only get to take one at a time, I love studying. I'm good at concentrating, all those years of having to tune out the chaos in my home to stay sane, I guess." A smile slowly crept over her face.

"I live in the cutest place. My apartment backs up to a creek. I can't afford one of the units right on the water, but I get to walk along the bank many evenings after work. That is truly one of my happy places.

"My landlords, Helen and Harold, are precious," she continued. "I'm very blessed to have them in my life. Helen and I always say we 'check on each other.' Harold plays golf every Saturday morning, so I'll drop in on her to see if she needs anything. If she sees me studying late, she often brings me snacks to keep me going. If my parents could have been anything like them, life would have been so different."

"Folks like that are a rare blessing," I agreed. "Natalie, I want you to write these things down and add everything you can think of to the list. Then read it three times a day for the next month. I think one of the best ways to keep from comparing yourself to others is to recount your own blessings. I want to see a copious and thorough list the next time you come in, okay?"

Natalie nodded.

"This verse has helped me not compare myself to other people," I said as I opened my Bible to Psalm 16. I shared verses 5 and 6, and then I asked her to write that verse at the top of her list of blessings so she could read it as often as she read her list. As an eager overachiever, Natalie readily agreed to her assignment.

Two weeks later, Natalie showed up for her appointment armed with her neatly typed, single-spaced, full-page list of what she had going for her. "After putting all this on paper, I realized that I really do have a lot going right," she said. "My boundary lines have fallen in pleasant places." She had continued reading the list daily, even though her boss informed her during this same period that raises were frozen in her department.

Natalie's list of blessings became the backbone of her healing. It kept her focus positive, enabling her to deal with the issues of her past and find the recovery she desired. Not long after she started counseling, she showed up to her appointment with a story she needed to tell.

"You remember Helen?" she asked.

"Your landlady?"

"That's her. Well, a couple of weeks ago, after my walk on Saturday, something told me to go and check on her. I discovered that she had fallen and had been trying to reach the phone. Clearly, her leg was broken, so I called 911 and stayed with her until help got there."

"Helen told me, 'I was crying out to God for help when you walked in!' Then she kept thanking me, saying she didn't know what she would have done without me."

Natalie continued, her eyes widening, "You're not going to believe what these awesome people have done. I went to see Helen in the hospital. She said that since she is going to need physical therapy after she leaves the hospital, she and Harold have decided to relocate to an assisted living center. They are subletting their apartment to me for a year—rent free! They just want someone to watch over the place in case they want to return when Helen is better.

"She handed me the keys and said, 'Now, dear, without having rent to pay, you can go to school full-time and finish your degree.' Can you believe how kind they are?"

Natalie's eyes filled with tears. "Linda, their apartment is right on the creek. I can sit at my kitchen table and watch the water trickling by. I can work part-time at a job that doesn't stress me out and focus on my classes. With some effort, I can finish in a year. This isn't just a blessing—it's a miracle!"

Despite the fact that her co-workers seemed to be blessed when she wasn't, God was preparing a "delightful inheritance" for her all along!

Polish Your Jewels

- Write out a list of all God has given you.

- Read your list every day and thank God for all you do have.

- Commit Psalm 16:5-6 to memory and read it every time you are tempted to compare yourself to someone else.

Day 7: Unexpected Blessing

As for God, his way is perfect;
    the word of the Lord is flawless.
He is a shield
    for all who take refuge in him.
For who is God besides the Lord?
    And who is the Rock except our God?
It is God who arms me with strength
    and makes my way perfect. (Psalm 18:30–32)

Scripture Insight: Because I'm not omniscient like God, it's not always easy for me to believe that things are going to work out. From my limited point of view, life can appear to be anything but perfect. You would think that after knowing God all these years, I would relax and take refuge in him, but it's easier said than done. Stories like this certainly help my faith along.

Mary Helen's Move

In 1988, Mary Helen and Pat were serving God as teachers at Christian school in Arizona when the school board voted to close the high school. Their daughter, Melinda, was just finishing her junior year and she was clearly unhappy about the board's choice.

Needing jobs, the couple sent out résumés through the Christian school network. Their search landed them with three job possibilities, all in Southern California—Escondido, Costa Mesa, and Thousand Oaks. After interviews with the schools, they were offered jobs in all three places! With prayerful consideration they decided Escondido was the place to go—much to Melinda's disappointment.

Amidst the hair-flipping and the door-slamming, the high school junior pleaded for her parents to leave her behind in Arizona.

"I lovingly explained that was not an option," Mary Helen shared. "'We are a family,' I told her, 'and families stick together.' But after a few more dramatic displays and crying spells, I almost *wanted* to leave her in Arizona!"

They put the house on the market and began the process of packing and preparing to move to California. A lot of people came to look at the house, but after a month they still had no viable offers.

On a Saturday morning in the midst of this process, Mary Helen got a call from the principal of the school in Escondido. He regretfully informed her that, due to a decline in enrollment, he had to retract the offers for their employment.

"I understand," Mary Helen told the apologetic man, "God's in charge." But inside, she panicked. *What are we going to do, Lord? We need jobs,* she prayed.

When her husband got home, they remembered that they had other offers so they decided to call the administrator in Thousand Oaks. After a half hour conversation, they made arrangements to travel there to finalize their contracts and begin looking for a place to live.

Just as Pat hung up the phone, it rang again. A man on the other end said, "I'm sure you don't remember me, but we looked at your house a week ago. We want to buy it." The couple sat next to the phone in awe at how God was clearly leading them.

A few days later, Mary Helen got a call from an old college roommate named Jois. She and her husband Alan were in the area and they wanted to meet for dinner. As they sat visiting, Mary Helen asked, " What are you two doing these days?"

Jois responded, " I'm an executive secretary for a law firm and Alan is an executive for a large automobile manufacturing company just outside of Thousand Oaks." Mary Helen couldn't believe her ears! They already had friends in the community where they were moving.

The move to Southern California went smoothly. Pat and Mary Helen were teaching and the kids were involved in school activities. Even Melinda was happy. By October she had met George, the man she would eventually marry.

When Melinda graduated from high school, she went to work at the law firm where Jois worked. Jois had no children, so she took a real interest in her. More than once she handed her a credit card and told her to go buy $200 worth of clothes for work!

Two years later, when Melinda was planning a wedding, Jois told Pat and Mary Helen that said she wanted the privilege of helping to pay for the wedding! By themselves, a couple of Christian school teachers could not have afforded the kind of wedding they were able to provide for Melinda.

"Only God could have woven such a beautiful tapestry out of all these threads that came together in one place at one time," Mary Helen said. "His plan is so perfect."

Polish Your Jewels

- If God helps his servants like Mary Helen and Pat, do you believe he will help you too?

- Write your name in the blanks and take ownership of Psalm 18:30-32 as a personal promise to you: "As for God, his way is perfect; the word of the Lord is flawless. He is a shield for _____ who takes refuge in him. For who is God besides the Lord? And who is the Rock except our God? It is God who arms _____ with strength and makes _____'s way perfect."

Day 8: Transformation

Who can discern his errors?
> Forgive my hidden faults.
Keep your servant also from willful sins;
> may they not rule over me.
Then will I be blameless,
> innocent of great transgression.
May the words of my mouth and the meditation of
my heart
> be pleasing in your sight,
O LORD, my Rock and my Redeemer.

(Psalm 19:12–14)

....

Scripture Insight: My friends in Christ-centered recovery have taught me so much. I want to know more about following God's plan, but they desire that knowledge enough to diligently seek it everyday. My investment in obeying God's statutes, precepts, and commands (to use the terminology of Psalms) pales in comparison to my friends who depend on God for sanity and sobriety. Their constant attitude of contrition and confession is worthy of imitation by all who profess Christ. From these faithful followers, I am learning to seek God one day at a time, and to please my Lord with every word and every action.

Colorful Casey Wayne

Casey Wayne was a mess. He had spent twenty-six years as an angry alcoholic, leaving much human carnage in his path of broken relationships. When he hit his bottom, he was ready to do whatever it took to make the pain go away. He turned his life over to the Lord and showed up at a recovery meeting or a church service nearly every night. When he said yes to Christ, he meant it. He joined a small group, attended men's Bible studies, and looked up everyone he had wronged so he could make amends.

"I asked my ex-wife to forgive me for all of those drunken nights and for wasting all of our money on booze. She actually did," he shared with his small group. "I don't know if I could forgive someone for doing what I did to her and the kids. Margaret is a Christian now too. She said that she forgave me back when she gave her life to Jesus. I can see him in her eyes."

That proud, selfish man who once bullied his family was quickly disappearing. He had asked God to be in charge now, and the Lord took him up on his offer. Now Casey was living his dream. This was the life of sobriety he always wished for in his moments of clarity.

Three months after his conversion, he woke up to what he thought would be the worst week of his life. His nineteen-year-old son got picked up for DUI.

"I blame myself for most of my son's trouble." Casey Wayne confided to his small group leader. "I wasn't parenting him. I was at the bottom of a bottle trying to medicate my own pain." However, he tried not to succumb to guilt.

Two days later, Casey found out that his dad had prostate cancer. The same day, his company told him they were laying off eight drivers, including him.

Casey's Bible study group was going through Philippians. That night for the first time he read Philippians 4:6–7: "Do not be anxious about anything, but in everything, by prayer and petition, with thanksgiving, present your requests to God. And the peace of God, which transcends all understanding, will guard your hearts and your minds in Christ Jesus."

When his group began discussing "prayer and petition," he felt he needed to do that. "I didn't have anything to lose except my heavy heart. We all prayed and I gave the Lord my burdens. I couldn't believe how much peace I had, knowing God could handle it all. I didn't have to make myself crazy worrying about all that stuff. In the past that would have made me drink! Now instead of filling up on booze, I'm filled with the Holy Ghost."

Letting God have his burden was a life-changing blessing. Casey was amazed by the answers God provided. His stepmother bought a ticket for him to see his dad. "And if I hadn't gotten laid off work, I wouldn't have had the time to go," he marveled.

Casey was with his dad just after surgery. In the days that followed, he had a chance to ask his father for forgiveness for the shame his alcohol brought to his family over the years. His dad begged for Casey's forgiveness, too, for being emotionally absent and for being so hard on him.

When Casey Wayne left, his dad looked him in the eye and said for the first time he could remember, "I love you, Son, and I'm proud of you."

One of the guys from his small group offered him a part-time job that could eventually become a full-time position. "Part-time was just what God wanted for me during that time, because the judge ordered my son to go to ninety recovery meetings in ninety days. I was available to take him to some meetings with me. He says he can see how I've changed for the better. Now he's asking me all kinds of questions about God. I think it's only a matter of time before he realizes his higher power is Jesus," Casey beamed.

"I don't want to screw this up, so every day I take a ruthless personal inventory and ask God to forgive my hidden faults. For years, I used my words to hurt people. Now I understand that I wanted to keep them at arm's length because I was hurting so badly," he confessed.

"God has truly become my strength. Now, instead of using my words to hurt other people, I pray every day what David in the Bible prayed: Let 'the words of my mouth and the meditation of my heart be pleasing in your sight, O Lord, my Rock and my Redeemer.'"

Polish Your Jewels

- Ask the Lord each day to forgive your hidden faults.

- Pray daily, "May the words of my mouth and the meditation of my heart be pleasing in your sight, O Lord, my Rock and my Redeemer."

- Learn Psalm 141:3: "Post a guard at my mouth, God. Set a watch at the door of my lips." Allow God to do this so that your words can be pleasing to him.

Day 9: Got Faith

Now I know that the LORD saves his anointed;
   he answers him from his holy heaven
   with the saving power of his right hand.
Some trust in chariots and some in horses,
   but we trust in the name of the LORD our God.

(Psalm 20:6–7)

....

Scripture Insight: In today's world, we worship self-sufficiency, but recent economic problems have challenged that ideal. Even our most educated financial decisions may not yield the results we expect. That brings us to our knees and we learn to focus on our God, not our 401K.

The Last Supper

Debbie and Jim won't be shaken by a gloomy economy. They learned early in their marriage where to place their trust.

Like so many young families, Debbie and Jim often found there was "too much month at the end of the money." With two small children, they both felt it was a priority for Debbie to stay home to raise them. That left Jim solely responsible for earning their income, a job he took on with pride and determination.

"I never wanted to make my husband feel bad," Debbie reported. "Jim was a hard worker. I knew he was doing the best he could, so I said nothing about our lack of food until I couldn't hide it any more."

That night as he walked in the door, Debbie used a sense of humor to let Jim know how broke they were: "This evening's dinner has a name, dear. We're going to call it 'the last supper'! Because that is what it is—the last of the food in the house. You can check the refrigerator and all you will see is the light. Check the freezer; all we have is ice. Look in the pantry and you'll see a six ounce can of tomato paste. That's it. That's all we have left!"

"The last supper, huh?" Jim chuckled.

They had been faithful to tithe, even though things were tight. Jim had worked as hard he could, and Debbie was careful with every penny. So they had been faithful in every respect.

As they bowed their heads to pray over dinner, Jim's face showed no sign of worry. He had no furrowed brow or worried words, just a heartfelt prayer of thanks for the food that was on the table.

They finished their meager dinner and busied themselves with their evening chores—doing dishes, bathing the kids, taking out the trash. Just as they were heading for bed, there was a knock at the door.

"It's ten o'clock at night. Who could that be?" Debbie wondered out loud.

She answered the door and a man asked, "Do you still have that coffee table you were selling at your yard sale a couple of weeks ago?"

"As a matter of fact, we do," she responded.

"I'll give you $40 for it!"

"Sold!"

Without wasting a minute, Debbie was in the car and at the Safeway store, filling her cart with milk, bread, eggs and the rest of what they needed to tide them over until payday.

Polish Your Jewels

- Think back over the landscape of your life to a time when God unmistakably answered your prayers. Does remembering God's conscientious care strengthen your faith now?

- Write out your story and share it with at least one other person to help build their faith.

Day 10: Trust

The LORD is my shepherd, I shall not be in want.
    He makes me lie down in green pastures,
he leads me beside quiet waters,
    he restores my soul.
He guides me in paths of righteousness
    for his name's sake.
Even though I walk
    through the valley of the shadow of death,
I will fear no evil,
    for you are with me;
your rod and your staff,
    they comfort me. (Psalm 23:1–6)

Scripture Insight: Using this timeless text, Bishop Ken Ulmer eloquently explained to three thousand pastors and their wives how our "sheepishness" can rob us of the peace God provides. Comparing us to sheep, he pointed out that God "makes" us lie down in green pastures because he knows we will trot right past our rest and peace if we aren't careful. That describes me to a T.

Sometimes I not only miss the rest he offers me today, but I will waste valuable time fretting over the future that God has well in-hand. This scripture assures me that even if life requires that I "walk through the valley of the shadow of death," God will protect me with his rod and guide me with his staff. All the while, even in the most challenging of circumstances, he will bring me comfort as I put my faith in him.

Bogus Beliefs

Gus, our loyal and faithful Labrador mix, was the best dog we ever had, but he didn't start out that way. My daughter Sarah spotted a skinny red ball of fur and energy wandering around the high school, so she coaxed Gus into her car. He was so hungry, a smashed sandwich left over from the previous week's lunch did the trick. Then she deposited him in our front yard to make it seem as though he just showed up there. She knew the whole family would fall for the lovable lug and he would find a good home. She was right. His enthusiasm and devotion won us over, and he quickly became a member of the family.

However, Gus brought a lot of bad habits we had to work on. He chased cars, tore into trash cans, and didn't come right away when we called. Worst of all, he constantly tormented the neighbor's sheep.

Since he loved to run, I decided to take him with me to burn off some of his excess energy as I made a few laps around the streets of our rural neighborhood. The houses in our area are widely spaced, and many of our neighbors took advantage of their acreage by raising horses or sheep.

The horses were too much of a challenge for Gus, but not the sheep. They seemed to be just the right size to "play" with him. Gus would charge into their pen despite loud protests from me and pounce near the weak creatures hoping to get a response. In reality, he wouldn't hurt them, but they didn't know that. His intimidating size and boisterous manner struck fear in their poor little sheep hearts.

I tried countless ways to discourage this behavior—speaking sternly, offering him bribes, even rapping him on the nose. Nothing dissuaded him from his new woolly friends. Whenever we ran near the pen, the sheep would bleat as though they were being beaten. They created so much commotion, they could be heard in the next county. Once he jumped the fence into the pen and several sheep that were gathered in a group simply fell to the ground. Gus merely walked toward them and they slumped in a lifeless heap.

Watching that reminded me of how I often respond to the devil's tricks. When life circumstances appear formidable, Satan whispers, "You're not going to make it through this." Or, "Where's God now? Why would he let this happen to you? I thought God loved you. You call this love?"

Like the sheep, I bleat with fear over something that isn't going to hurt me because God won't let it. Sometimes I'm tempted to lie down and quit like my fearful animal friends. I want to crawl into bed and pull the covers over my head in despair. I've even seen some fretful folks believe Satan's lies and give up on God all together. They forget that we're *God's* sheep and he loves us perfectly. Whatever happens in our lives, he can work it out for good. (Romans 8:28)

Referring to 1 Peter 5:8, my former pastor used to say, "Satan may go around like a roaring lion, looking for someone to devour. But the best he can do is gum you to death—if you let him."

Verse 9 of that same passage says to "resist him, standing firm in the faith." We don't have to lie down and give up like the sheep. We can resist the devil and, James 4:7 tells us, he will flee. To quote my former pastor again, "It doesn't say he will stroll, or saunter, or mosey. The scripture tells us that when we stand strong in the faith, believing God, *Satan will flee.*"

The tortured creatures in my neighborhood would have benefited to know that Gus was harmless. Likewise, we benefit every day by knowing the truth of God's Word: God's will won't take us where his grace can't keep us.

Polish Your Jewels

- Set aside some time in prayer to identify the lies Satan wants you to believe. Notice the falsehoods about you personally. What fear does he try to plant about your future? What guilt does he use to keep you stuck in the past?

- Now prayerfully recognize God's truth about each concern and answer each of Satan's lies with that truth.

- Ask God to bring that truth to your recollection when Satan wants to sell you a case of bogus beliefs.

Day 11: Divine Parenting

When my father and mother forsake me,
   then the LORD will take me up" (Psalm 27:10 KJV)

....

Scripture Insight: I love the way the King James Version puts this verse. When it says that the Lord will "take me up," it conjures the image of a kind, cuddly granny who pulls you into her lap and rocks you until your tank is full of comfort.

I didn't have a granny around or even a dad after I was five, and my mom stayed busy and angry about it most of the time. I hardly have a memory of her nurturing my siblings or me. But there have been times in my life when the presence of God was so palpable, I could feel him reassuring me in a way far beyond any parent could. When parents can't do the job of caring for their kids as God intends, he often takes their place.

Daddy's Lap

Suzanne made an appointment for counseling when the doctors informed her that breast cancer had returned. At only thirty-three, she was dealing with this challenge again. She had battled cancer in her early twenties just after her beautiful daughter, Katie, was born.

"I made it through cancer last time fighting everyday just to get out of bed," she informed me. "The strong chemo kicked me to the curb every morning, but I had to keep going because Katie needed her mom. I trusted God to get me through when I didn't know what was ahead of me. If I had known at the time the places my cancer would take me, I would have imploded. Now I know exactly what I'm facing and it's much harder to muster the faith."

"Let's talk about your worst fears," I counseled. "Speaking them out helps to take their power away. Speaking them out to God brings his power to us."

We spent the rest of the hour looking at specific worries she had about her future. We found her Freeing Three, three Scripture passages that would bring her strength.[1] Then we agreed to meet each week to shore up her faith during this difficult time.

A couple of Sundays later, I sat in church several rows behind Suzanne. Sitting to her left was her mother, Lorraine, and to her right was her precious six-year-old, Katie. It was a particularly moving worship service, so both Suzanne and Lorraine had tears streaming down their cheeks. My heart went out to the young mother facing such a formidable diagnosis. I prayed for her and her family as they wept.

In an amazing mother moment I watched Lorraine reach out, wrap her arm around Suzanne, and pull her close. As Suzanne rested peacefully against her mother,

---

1. From *Twelve Ways to Turn Your Pain into Praise,* Linda Newton (Anderson, IN: Warner Press, 2008), 25. The exercise of the "Freeing Three" requires you to find three verses that address your need, post copies of them in three places, and read them three times a day for three weeks.

the serene look on her face was identical to the look on her little girl's face. It said, "I'm safe here. I'm okay while I'm in my mother's arms."

As I prayerfully observed this sacred moment, I thought, *I've never experienced a mother's love like that and I never will.* I burst into tears and looked for a way to leave the sanctuary and deal with my emotions in private.

But then I seemed to hear the Lord's still small voice, saying, "I'm here for you. You have my lap now and you will have it forever."

In my mind's eye, I could see Jesus standing before me with his arms outstretched. As I came toward him, I could feel him pull me in his lap, stroke my head and say, "It's okay. I've got you now. You're gonna be all right."

That wasn't the last time I crawled into the Lord's lap to find comfort and strength. Although I didn't have a mother who was capable of nurturing me, I'm glad to have an Abba Father who is available 24/7/365.

Polish Your Jewels

- Ask the Lord to fill any voids you experienced in the parenting you received.

- Recognize that Christ is now your spiritual parent. Praise him for that regularly.

- Crawl up in his lap often to find the comfort and strength you need.

Day 12: Let Go and Let God

You did it: you changed wild lament
    into whirling dance;
You ripped off my black mourning band
    and decked me with wildflowers.
I'm about to burst with song;
    I can't keep quiet about you.
God, my God,
    I can't thank you enough. (Psalm 30:11-12 MSG)

....

Scriptural Insight: "Let go and let God." You probably have
seen this slogan on wall plaques, T-shirts, and decorative
calendars. It makes a lot of sense. We are smart enough to
know that some things are too big for us to handle, and
we need to let God handle them for us. So why do we have
such a hard time letting him do that? Is it because we are
secretly afraid he won't do what we want? In the end, we
realize that he knows best, and his plan was the best one
all along. If understanding this truth could help us trust
him sooner, we might save ourselves a lot of grief.

Monumental Moments

I am continually grateful that God provides
opportunities for me to speak to his ladies. It's a task
I don't take lightly. I had been searching for a way

to help women attending my retreats to experience a definitive time of letting go of their burdens. I wanted to create what I called a "Monumental Moment" in my book *Twelve Ways to Turn Your Pain into Praise.*[1] In the Old Testament, when God did something memorable or miraculous for the children of Israel, he would instruct them to erect a monument to commemorate the event. The Lord wanted his people to do that so they wouldn't forget his goodness and provision. We can have those moments forever etched in time when we remember "doing business with God."

To create that, I searched for paper that would dissolve in water. My husband found some online. On Saturday evening at a retreat in the California foothills with a hundred ladies, I had several stations with large bowls of warm water set up. At the close of the session, I told the ladies, "You were given a sheet of paper when you came in. There are things you have been carrying around for way too long and the Lord brought you here this weekend so you can release your burden to him. Perhaps it's something you continue to wring your hands in worry over—perhaps a sin that you need to ask his forgiveness for or guilt over a sin you've already surrendered to the Lord but for which you can't forgive yourself. Perhaps there's resentment in your heart toward someone who has offended you. Maybe you're holding onto some resentment toward God because he didn't work things out the way you thought he should.

1. Newton, *Twelve Ways*, 259.

"You can take the time right now to write down on your paper what you want to let go of. Then, as you are ready, come and drop your piece of paper into the water and see it dissolve right before your eyes. This is your Monumental Moment in time when you will forever remember laying your burden down."

A quiet reverence enveloped the room as every lady made her way to a large bowl of water to watch her problem disappear. As I observed God at work, I felt like I was standing on holy ground.

The next morning at breakfast, a gentle lady in her late sixties asked if she could talk to me. Bobbie's face was radiant. I couldn't wait to hear what she had to say.

She sat down next to me with a cup of coffee and opened up. "Last night meant so much to me. You see, my dad was an alcoholic, and by the time I was nine, my mom couldn't handle it any more. Instead of just leaving him, she cheated on him and then left, taking me with her. After that she paraded countless boyfriends into our house until I couldn't deal with it any longer. I ran away when I was only fifteen. As punishment, I ended up in a girl's prison. They called it juvenile hall, but it was prison complete with crooked guards, tough chores, and angry inmates.

"After nine months, I was sent home. Nothing had changed, so I ran away again. I guess I figured that another nine months in girl's prison wasn't as bad as living with mom and her latest loser, so I was off again to 'juvenile hall.'

"I met George through one of the girls from prison. He was a charmer, but he had a hard time staying out of trouble. It wasn't long before his trouble landed him in prison. The minute he got out, I ran away with him to get married.

"As a married man, George was less than charming. He was an alcoholic, a womanizer, and a wife-beater. I finally questioned what I had gotten myself into, but by then we had three kids, the youngest only three weeks old, so I didn't know where else to go.

"I thank God that he placed a neighbor in my life to invite me to church," Bobbie continued. "I found the Lord when I was twenty-four years old, and he made all the difference. I hoped that George would welcome the change too. I prayed every day for him to turn his life over to God, but he didn't. A year after I came to Christ, George left us.

"Linda, I have prayed practically everyday since George left for God to send me another man to marry. My desire has made me miserable at times. I've begged God for forty years, but last night I let go of my longing and asked God to fulfill my life. After that wonderful service, I could hardly speak I was so filled with the Spirit. I am ready to embrace whatever he desires for my life now."

"I think you already are," I informed her. "I can see his love reflected in your face at this moment." We both smiled as we finished our coffee and basked in the Lord's lavish love.

Polish Your Jewels

- What do you need to let go of today?

- Write it down and then ceremonially destroy the paper as you surrender it to the Lord.

- Thank God for his deliverance.

Day 13: Provision

Taste and see that the LORD is good.
    Oh, the joys of those who take refuge in him!
Fear the LORD, you his godly people,
    for those who fear him will have all they need.
Even strong young lions sometimes go hungry,
    but those who trust in the LORD will lack no good
    thing. (Psalm 34: 8–10 NLT)

....

Scripture Insight: When we decide to walk in obedience
to the Lord, life isn't instantly tied up in a nice pink bow.
God's Word tells us that he will care for us, but he doesn't
always tell us how. Many times he waits till the last minute
to tell us anything. Still, God proves he is trustworthy.
Trusting him to provide our needs will bring us peace. I
don't know about you, but in these turbulent times, I can
use all the peace I can get.

Janine's Java

Janine was new to the church but not to the Christian
faith. She was raised in a Christian home, but teenage
turmoil caused her to wander away from a Christian
lifestyle as she searched for comfort in a bottle.

Thirty years and a broken marriage later, she met John
at a recovery meeting. A good man with several years of

recovery under his belt, he fell instantly in love with Janine, and he never failed to let her know it.

Four years after they were married, Janine decided to go back to church. In her twelve-step recovery program, she never doubted that her "higher power" was the Lord and she was now ready to reconnect with his people. Church had never been a part of John's life, so she thought he might resist the idea. But his love for Janine had him in the front row as soon as she asked.

A few months after he started attending Sierra Pines, John walked into the pastor's office and said, "How do you do that 'accept Jesus' thing?"

My husband Bruce said it was the easiest conversation he'd had with a seeker in thirty years of ministry. "The fruit just fell from the tree," he said.

Now that John had given his heart to the Lord, Janine brought up the idea of tithing. Employed in construction in his fifties, John worked hard for his money; as a hairdresser, Janine did as well. Together they made a commitment to return to God one tenth of the income he provided for them each week.

Several months passed. Like all of us, they found that it was easier to give their ten percent some weeks than other weeks. One Sunday, after writing out their tithe check, Janine realized they only had $4.71 in their checking account. "The only thing we really need is coffee," she explained to John. "Other than that, we have enough food in the house to tide us over until payday."

The couple decided to put their tithe check in the offering basket and trust God to provide for them.

After church they were walking to the car when Janine realized she needed to stop at the church office and drop off an announcement for the newsletter.

Bruce was talking to the administrator when Janine walked into the office. Just as she laid her announcement on the secretary's desk, a gentleman opened the door and handed Bruce a bag. "This is for you, Pastor. My wife didn't like it."

"I didn't care for it, either," Bruce laughed. "That's why I gave it to you! Here, let's give it to Janine."

The gentleman handed Janine a bag of coffee.

Polish Your Jewels

- Has God ever unmistakably provided for you?

- Write down all that he did to take care of you and how you *felt* as you witnessed his provision.

- When you grow impatient waiting for God to provide for your needs, overlay those past feelings of faith and strength onto your current situation. Let your past faith empower your present circumstances.

Day 14: Pliable

Delight yourself in the LORD
　　and he will give you the desires of your heart.
Commit your way to the LORD;
　　trust in him and he will do this:
He will make your righteousness shine like the dawn,
　　the justice of your cause like the noonday sun.

(Psalm 37:4–6)

....

Scripture Insight: The Old Testament's Hebrew language has several terms that our English versions translate with the word *delight*. In Esther 6:6, when King Xerxes wanted to reward Mordecai for saving his life, he said, "What should be done for the man the king delights to honor?" In this verse, *delights* is the word used to translate *chephets* (pronounced, *khaw-fates*). It literally means "to be pleased with."

Psalm 119:77 reads, "Let your compassion come to me that I may live, for your law is my delight." The word for *delight* in this verse translates the Hebrew *shashua* (pronounced, *shah-shoo-ah*). It means "enjoyment" or "pleasure."

A third Hebrew word is used for *delight* in Psalm 37:4. This is the Hebrew word *anag*, (pronounced, *aw-nag*). It means to be soft and pliable. This tells me that when I "delight" in the Lord, I allow myself to be molded and shaped by him. When I surrender my will to his, he offers me salvation, satisfaction, purpose, and fulfillment—the true desires of my heart.

What Really Matters

Just after college, my husband and I went into youth ministry. We soon found that working in a church was challenging and certain church folks less than kind, so we decided to take a year off from ministry. That one year off turned into eight, and before long we had more money than we knew what to do with. Our accountant insisted we invest in real estate, so we decided to buy our dream home in Oregon.

On an evening in late summer, a few months after we moved in, we sat on the deck admiring the view. Bruce turned to me and said, "Sure is beautiful, isn't it?"

"Sure is."

"Sure worked hard to get here, didn't we?"

"Sure did."

Just as I was thinking it, Bruce said, "Sure is empty, isn't it?"

"Sure is." Neither of us knew what to do with those feelings, so we quickly changed the subject.

Less than a year later, our third child was born. A routine check-up when she was ten days old resulted in a frantic trip to the hospital five hours north of our home. Our precious new baby girl, Ashley Rose, had to have emergency heart surgery. By the grace of God, she survived, but we were told she would need many more surgeries in her life.

Now I had the daunting task of taking care of my post-operative baby without the benefit of qualified doctors and nurses. As we pulled into driveway of the home I thought I could never live without, I was aware of suddenly how little it meant to me. I just wanted my baby to be all right.

Because her heart was so weak, Ashley's immune system was compromised. So she spent most of her early years in the hospital. Bruce had been on the road for the past year doing sales and promotion, but now he couldn't muster the gumption to leave again. "Suppose she gets sick while I'm gone and, God forbid,…" Neither of us wanted to finish his sentence.

So my husband got off the road, and we had to generate income by selling things. First went the antiques—those precious pieces that I spent hours procuring. At one time they meant so much to me, but now all I thought was, *Take them, Lord. Take the 1850s hand-painted Waterbury clock. Take the walnut dresser and the Persian rug. Just let me keep my baby.*

Then it was our motor home, followed by the Jeep CJ. *I don't care about losing these things, Lord,* I prayed. *I just don't want to lose my Ashley.*

Finally, we had to sell the house. It was my pride and joy. I'm embarrassed to recall how many hours I spent hovering over designer magazines, selecting just the right wallpaper and color schemes, fretting over what my friends would think about my décor. When the house sold, I didn't care. With the real estate market depressed, we didn't net a dime out of the sale, but at least we got out from under the mortgage payment. And we still had our baby girl.

As I was packing up our household goods, Bruce posed a question: "Honey, since we're obviously going to be poor, do you want to be poor for God again?"

If he had asked me that one year earlier, I would have laughed in his face. But in the months after Ashley's birth, I had spent a lot of time on my knees and I was hearing from the Lord again. "Why not?" I replied. "At least if we're in ministry, we'll have purpose in the midst of our poverty."

So my husband and I packed up our little family and moved six hundred miles to a church that paid us $500 a month and a house that rented for $450. Every month, God miraculously provided for the rest of our needs through the loving people in our church family.

My husband was the music minister and we taught a large young adult Sunday school class. We hadn't been there long when a couple in the class threw a party for the whole group. One of the dear ladies who worked in the church nursery insisted on taking care of our kids so we could attend.

It was a wonderful evening of fun and fellowship—until 8:30 that night. We got a call from the babysitter saying, "I don't know what happened. Ashley was playing just fine until she crawled up in my lap and went limp. I felt her head and she's burning up."

Bruce and I left the party, picked up Ashley, and rushed to the children's hospital. The emergency room doctor suspected an infection. Ashley was so fragile that the doctor told us to stay at the hospital for a few hours in case she reacted to the medication he prescribed.

It was already late on Saturday night. "Honey, there's no need for both of us to lose a night's sleep," I told Bruce. "You have to work at church tomorrow, so why don't you get the older kids from the sitter and head home? I'll stay with Ashley." He conceded.

I told the attending nurse I was going to step outside for a minute to get a breath of fresh air. She nodded as I walked out of the waiting room with my lethargic baby in my arms. Overwhelmed with emotion, I exclaimed, "OK, Satan, you take your best shot. You have taken everything—the cars, the toys, the house, and now you want to take our daughter. Well, even if you take Ashley, I will not turn my back on God. Do you hear me? I'm in this for the long haul. Even if she's gone, I will not turn my back on God!"

At that very moment, my precious Ashley woke up in my arms, saying, "Hungry, mommy."

We left the hospital that night. In the days and weeks that followed, I watched Ashley gain weight and grow stronger.

That hot, sticky night in the hospital parking lot, I had learned that when we delight ourselves in the Lord, he becomes our heart's desire.

Polish Your Jewels

- Have you ever found yourself mindlessly pursuing an imperfect plan for your life?

- How did you make a course correction?

- What can you do today to be more pliable to God's plan for you?

Day 15: Beggars Can Be Choosers

The LORD directs the steps of the godly.
>He delights in every detail of their lives.
Though they stumble, they will never fall,
>for the LORD holds them by the hand.
Once I was young, and now I am old.
>Yet I have never seen the godly abandoned,
>or seen their children begging for bread.

>(Psalm 37:23–25 NLT)

....

Scripture Insight: This is one of my favorite promises in Psalms. It tells me that God delights in every detail of my life—even little things that are of no eternal consequence, although they matter to me.

When I read the second part of this verse to women's groups, I add this comment: "Once I was young, and now I am old—but I prefer young." It gets laughs because women can identify with the feeling. The truth is, I'm okay with getting older as long as I know the Lord is delighting in me and holding my hand.

This verse promises that God will not forsake me or the precious children he's given me to love. This promise puts my heart to rest.

Shelley's Celebration

Shelley's world collapsed when her husband walked out on her and the two boys. "I don't know what I'm going to do," she sobbed, sitting on the plaid sofa of my office. "Eric's moved in with this secretary. She's practically a child. Josh and Ryan are crushed and want nothing to do with their dad. He keeps inviting them over, and he's clueless as to why they won't come. Can't he see that they feel betrayed? Are they just supposed to go over and hang out at Dad's with his girlfriend and act like nothing happened? What's he thinking?"

"He's not thinking. That's the problem," I said. I referred her to a comment from Willard Harley's book *His Needs, Her Needs* that says that a guy's brain turns to mush when he's having an affair.

"I feel so inadequate. I've been traded in for a newer model because I've got too many miles on me, miles that I logged taking care of Eric."

I nodded. Her honesty was helping her get to the root of her issues. Denying her feelings would only make them fester.

"I'll have to sell the house, and it's the only home the boys have known. Then I'll have to go to work. I haven't had a job in ten years. Eric never wanted me to work so I would have time to run his errands and make home-cooked meals. So I dutifully complied—for all the good it did me." She drew a ragged breath and kept rolling.

"Linda, why did God let this happen? He could have made Eric wake up."

"I believe God tried. When Eric comes out of his 'love coma,' if he's being honest, he will admit that God tried to get through to him."

I explained, "Shelley, God is limited by only one thing. He's not limited by evil. He's limited only by our will, because he loves us enough to let us choose how we live. I believe he goes to great lengths to help us choose wisely, but ultimately we make our own choices. Eric made his choice, and it is not without consequences."

Looking intently at her, I said, "You don't have to make the boys see their dad if they don't want to. Don't fuel their fire by running down their dad, but don't tell them they *have* to see their father either. Eric has earned their disapproval. It will take time to win back their favor, if he ever does. In the meantime, you are going to take care of yourself. You've made a career out of caring for everyone else. Now it's time to put yourself on that list.

"It's okay to be angry with God right now because that's how you honestly feel. 'Have your fit and fall in it,' as we say in the South, but be ready to move on because this situation is not God's fault. The best friend you have right now is the Lord. We're going to spend the rest of this hour praying through those angry feelings so you can embrace his power and peace for the days ahead."

I led Shelley through a prayer exercise to dump her baggage of resentment, grief, and self-loathing. A smile began to emerge from all of those tears.

"We have more bags to unpack," I informed her, "but this should start you on you path to healing."

"I feel tired, but lighter."

"Shelley, I have a word of caution for you," I said as we concluded our session. "Since you are dealing with anger toward Eric, questioning God, and needing to prove you are still a desirable woman, it would be easy to go out and do something stupid that you will regret forever. That would blow up your life. You would not believe how many good Christian women have such momentary lapses in judgment at times like these. Hang in there. You will feel better sooner than you think."

"After our prayer, I'm already feeling better," she said.

"Before you leave, I want to give you a promise from God." I then read Psalm 37:23–25 (NLT): "The steps of the godly are directed by the Lord. He delights in every detail of their lives. Though they stumble, they will not fall, for the Lord holds them by the hand. Once I was young, and now I am old. Yet I have never seen the godly forsaken, nor seen their children begging for bread."

"This verse was written just for me and my boys," Shelley said.

"I totally agree. I want you post these three powerful verses in three places, and read them three times a day for three weeks. I call that the Freeing Three. Satan wants to tell us lies about the future, but the Bible tells us the truth. Jesus said the truth sets us free."

Shelley stayed the course. She continued to come to church and keep our counseling appointments, staying focused on Christ. She even joined a women's Bible study and let the ladies of the church show their love for her. I saw her the day after Eric decided to show up at Ryan's soccer game with his new main squeeze. "Ryan was so upset, he left the field without speaking a word to his dad," Shelley said. "Eric accused me of putting him up to that. He still doesn't get the damage he's doing. Thank God for the ladies in my group who let me cry and prayed for me."

One of the women in her Bible study helped her get a part-time job. Another watched Josh until Ryan got home from high school. "It's certainly not easy, but I do feel like God is directing my steps," Shelley admitted one afternoon in counseling. "The promise you gave me in Psalms has become my life verse. I put it up all over the house. I've read it so much that I have the whole thing committed to memory.

"The first day of my new job, I kept repeating Philippians 4:13: 'I can do all things through Christ who strengthens me.' When Eric quit giving us money, I wanted call up and give him a piece of my mind, but I realized he wouldn't get it and I would make myself crazy. Instead I quoted Philippians 4:19: 'And my God will meet all your needs according to his glorious riches in Christ Jesus.' When I started dating a guy from work way too soon, I heard the words of my psalm echo in my head: 'Though they stumble, they will not fall, for the Lord holds them by the hand.'"

Shelley remained faithful. Three years after Eric left, she met Ed, a wonderful Christian man, when they attended the same small group at church. He fell in love with her and her sons. They were married a year later.

Shelley looked stunning at the wedding. At the reception, she came over to my table and gave me a big hug. Beaming from ear to ear, she said, "God is so good, Linda." I knew exactly what she meant.

Polish Your Jewels

- Journal details about the times God has demonstrated that he delights in every detail of your life—e.g., an item you have been shopping for shows up on the clearance rack; the class you need to take this semester opens up on the only night you have free; you receive a refund check from the IRS when you were fully expecting to owe them more.

- Do you trust God to take care of you and your children, or do you find yourself meddling with his plans?

- Read Psalm 37:23 often to remind yourself that you're not in charge.

Day 16: Patience

I waited patiently for the LORD;
    he turned to me and heard my cry.
He lifted me out of the slimy pit,
    out of the mud and mire;
he set my feet on a rock
    and gave me a firm place to stand.
He put a new song in my mouth,
    a hymn of praise to our God. (Psalm 40:1–3)

Scripture Insight: A phrase in this passage is so significant, so profound, and if we are not careful, we will read right past these four amazing words: *He turned to me.* Stop just for a moment and let this soak in. The Lord God—the Creator of everything you see around you, the One who placed every star in the night, the One who knows every grain of sand on every beach—turned to you. (Write your name here: _____.) He turned to the person sitting in your seat.

I didn't have parents who turned to me. My dad was gone by the time I was five. My mom was a working single mother with four kids. I can count on one hand the times she actually stopped to hear what I had to say. But God turns to me and hears my cry. It may take the rest of my life for me to wrap my mind around the magnitude of this. In the meantime, I will simply rejoice in it.

God's Waiting Room

When I was twelve years old, I said yes to Jesus Christ at a little country church near Chattanooga, Tennessee. My parents weren't Christians. They weren't even together at the time. After my dad left, Mom started waiting tables during the dinner shift at a local restaurant. With no parents at home, I received little instruction on how to live. If it wasn't for the church, I would have been lost.

On Sunday mornings, I could watch folks living together as families. At first, it was strange to see dads with their kids and moms embracing those dads, but I learned that's what healthy family connections looked like. Not only did I see good examples in the church service, but I learned at youth group what God said in his Word about relationships.

Richard, my youth pastor, explained the problem with being unequally yoked as he read 2 Corinthians 6:14–16, "Do not be yoked together with unbelievers. For what do righteousness and wickedness have in common? Or what fellowship can light have with darkness? What harmony is there between Christ and Belial? What does a believer have in common with an unbeliever? What agreement is there between the temple of God and idols? For we are the temple of the living God. As God has said: 'I will live with them and walk among them, and I will be their God, and they will be my people.'"

Richard continued, "As Christians, we believe that God is the center of who we are. If you can't share the most important thing in your life with the single most significant person to you, you'll feel empty and lonely. Besides, if your spouse doesn't share your values, you'll end up in a lot of arguments."

Richard also taught us about saving ourselves for marriage. "God wants you to stay pure because he has someone special for each of you to share your life with. Sexual intimacy is a gift from God, and it's intended for the person who will be there for all your tomorrows, not just for a good time tonight."

Richard's words made sense to me. It wasn't easy to wait on God when I saw so many of my friends caving in to the culture. But I had a firsthand view of how destructive marriage could be without the Lord, so I hung on.

Through nothing short of a miracle, God enabled me to go to a Christian college. There were young people like me, also struggling to figure out God's plan for their lives.

I was taking psychology courses and one day in class we were reading about Sigmund Freud's theory of "repetition compulsion," which states that a person will actively engage in behavior that mimics an earlier stressor, either deliberately or unconsciously. Freud believed that, even though a certain behavior could be destructive for us, we are compelled to repeat what is familiar to us.

My professor, who was also a counselor, explained that he had seen women who had married two or three alcoholic husbands. While they lamented how destructive their relationships were, they expressed how drawn they were to other drunks. As my professor explored their family of origin, he uncovered that in each case, daddy had been an alcoholic. If they had had a stepfather, he was too. These women didn't like the chaos of alcoholism, but they felt comfortable there.

He assigned a reading in our textbook that detailed additional cases with even more destructive behavior, in which people consciously or subconsciously willed to repeat their problems because of past trauma. With each new case study, I became more and more aware of how vulnerable I was.

I face-planted myself on the carpet in my second-floor dorm room. As I lay prostrate before the Lord, I begged him not to let me choose someone who would be toxic for me. I asked the Lord to make me conscious of my choices and to "stab me awake" (to quote author Howard Hendricks) if I was headed in the wrong direction.

As I cried out to the Lord in the loneliness of that dorm room, I sensed that he heard my cry. I was awash in his comfort and assurance. As I promised to listen to the Lord, he promised to guide me.

Four years later, I woke up early for my wedding day and the Lord brought that precious prayer time to mind. As I reflected on Bruce, my soon-to-be husband, I realized how profoundly God had answered that prayer. Bruce was a kind, compassionate man who loved the Lord and wanted deeply to please him. Due to my psychological trauma, I could have selected an angry, abandoning abuser, but my groom possessed the patience of Job. Bruce was capable enough to lead me, but smart enough to do it gently.

That combination has worked for the past thirty-four years. God has been good to me. He turned to me and answered my prayer.

Polish Your Jewels

- Stop and reflect for a moment on the fact that almighty God turns to you.

- Thank him for his attentiveness and let him know your heart's cry.

- Stay faithful to him in prayer and reading his Word.

- Watch how he lifts you out of the mire of confusion and plants your feet on stable ground.

Day 17: Divine Appointment

Many, O LORD my God,
 are the wonders you have done.
The things you planned for us
 no one can recount to you;
were I to speak and tell of them,
 they would be too many to declare. (Psalm 40:5)

Scripture Insight: Now and then, I get a divine nudge, an overwhelming notion that God is leading me to do something specific for him. I can hardly get my head around the idea that the Creator of the universe, the Everlasting God wants to use me.

Daniel Wallace, author of *Who's Afraid of the Holy Spirit,* calls the urging of the Holy Spirit, "an inarticulate impulse." I am trying to fine-tune the frequency of my heart so that I can recognize God's inarticulate impulse.

Long-Awaited Healing

I love speaking at women's retreats, although giving four to five talks in less than forty-eight hours can be demanding. That's why I seldom set up private counseling sessions with attendees, even though I love counseling as much as I love speaking. But on a weekend retreat high in the hills of Georgia, God had other plans.

I woke up early to prep my talk for Saturday morning, but during my prayer time I couldn't shake the idea that I should approach the retreat planner, Louise, about blocking off time to meet individually with some of the women attending. There had been no explicit requests from the women I met the evening before—just a strong impression that God wanted me to do this. The longer I've spent in the Lord's presence, the more I've learned to heed such impressions.

Louise was delighted with the idea. Without hesitation, she made an announcement during the morning session and set a sign-up sheet in the back of the room. It filled up right away. Before I had seen everyone on the list, I had confirmation that the idea indeed came from God. The first woman who sat down with me provided that proof.

Francine was a gentle lady in her sixties. I had just shared my testimony about my growing up in an abusive home and my inability to please my mom, no matter how hard I tried. With tears in her eyes, Francine said, "I had your mother too. They may have had different names, but they were the same person. Nothing I ever did was enough."

"I'm sorry," I replied.

"I think I'm a nice person, but my mother always said she wished she never had kids. I kills me just to say that to you, but she said it to my brother and me practically on a daily basis.

"When my three boys were small, I would take them over to see her and she would say terrible things to them too. She said, 'Little boys should be shot after they reach the age of six.' I finally stopped bringing them with me for their own protection. She's only gotten worse in her old age, and I can hardly stand to be around her negativity, but I don't know what to do with the guilt I feel for avoiding her."

Few people understand the dilemma of wanting to obey God by honoring a parent who is too toxic to be around, but I understood her plight. I had lived it as well.

"I am in awe of who God brings into my life, Francine. I understand your predicament, and I think I have an answer for you. May I read you a story about a woman named Lucille that will help illustrate it?" I read this story from my book *Twelve Ways to Turn Your Pain into Praise*:

Lucille spent her early years taking care of her mother. She and her brother, Stephen who was three years older, handled most everything, the meals, laundry and even her younger siblings, Julie and Travis, when they came along.

"Travis and Julie's father was the only man my mother ever loved, and she told that to anyone who would listen even if he wouldn't marry her. It became obvious to Stephen and me that mom treated the younger kids far differently than we were treated. Mom bought Travis a car when he was barely sixteen. He promptly wrecked it, and she went out and bought him another one. He wrecked that too. Julie never learned how to do life because every time she made a mess of things, mom came along with a broom to sweep it up. Julie was my only sister, and she started out so adorable. It broke my heart to watch her go down the tubes.

"I left home as soon as I could get out. My mom never forgave me. She sat home smoking joints with Julie and writing me letters about what a rotten daughter I was. It took three months of therapy to realize that I couldn't fix it, and another three months to understand that I wasn't a bad person.

"At my mom's funeral three years ago, I looked over at Stephen. He's a schoolteacher now, so handsome, and polite. He loves his kids and is active in his church. Then I looked at Ted, my husband, standing beside our four beautiful children. By God's grace, I married an amazing man. He works so hard all day, but still musters the energy to come home and involve himself with his family. He and I did a good job with our children.

"Then there was Julie in the corner seriously strung out on crank. She and mom had gotten into the harder stuff, and I think that contributed to mom's early death. Travis wasn't even there because he's doing time for possession of stolen property.

"As I stood by my mother's coffin, I had a lightning-bolt revelation from the Lord. What is it that we as parents want more than anything for our kids? We want them to grow up to be God-fearing, law-abiding, tax-paying citizens who take care of their families and live happy productive lives. In fact, that would honor us more than anything else our adult children could do. I realized as we stood there, that Stephen and I had done that. We brought honor to mom, but only because we were able to distance from her. If we had stayed close to home and continued the dysfunctional dance that mom wanted, like Julie and Travis did, that would not have happened."[1]

With tears streaming down her cheeks, Francine sobbed, "I get it, Linda. Lucille must have been reading my e-mail. My brother is a meth addict. He didn't break away from my mom either. I refused to stay that close to mom, or I would have become as messed up as he is. I was headed that way when I found Christ."

"You're fired from the guilt!"

Francine laughed through her tears, "I know." She heaved a sigh of relief while drying her eyes. "Linda, I have talked to counselors, pastors, and pastors wives for years for an answer for this. Today, I finally got one. Thank you for taking the time to meet with me."

"You're welcome, and you can thank the Lord. He had this planned all along. I'm just glad I was paying attention."

Polish Your Jewels

- Spend your quiet time not just speaking to the Lord. Set aside time in prayer to listen for his "inarticulate impulses."

---

1. Newton, *Twelve Ways*, 118–20.

- If you think God is speaking to you, check your impressions against his written Word. They will never be in conflict.

- If your inner prompting agrees with Scripture, follow through in obedience. The more we obey, the more God trusts us to be his hands and feet.

Day 18: Be Still

Be still, and know that I am God. (Psalm 46:10)

....

Scripture Insight: Old Testament Hebrew uses several words for *still*. When David says, "He leads me beside the *still* waters," in Psalm 23, the Hebrew word for *still* means "comfortable" or "quiet." The Hebrew word for *still* in Psalm 46:10 is *raphah,* which means "to cease," "to be idle," "to let go," or even "to draw toward evening" (like you're sitting on your front porch swing, with no agenda but to sip sweet tea and wait for the lightning bugs to show up). The root for *raphah* is the Hebrew word *rapha.* It means "to mend by stitching," "to heal or repair."

Even though I tend to be a Type A busy person, there have been times in my life, incredible God-moments, when I was able to slow down long enough for God to heal me. Moments like this one.

Real Southern Comfort

When my dad was admitted to the hospital for cancer surgery, I wanted to be by his side. I felt that a person going through a life-threatening surgery needed to be surrounded by family and friends, and that included me.

I jumped on the earliest flight I could get from Fresno to Charlotte and arrived just as he was coming out of surgery. When I walked into the waiting room, it was clear my step-mom, Barb, was exhausted. Watching over a sick patient in the hospital can be draining.

Within a few hours, my dad had moved from the post-surgery ICU to a room by himself. He was sleeping peacefully without all the machines and tubes he'd required just hours earlier.

"Barb, would you please go home and get some rest?" I suggested. "I'll stay with Daddy. I'm jet-lagged and I can't sleep anyway."

"I don't want to leave you here all by yourself."

"I'm used to hospital life. I'll be fine. But you won't if you don't get some sleep. They will have to clear a hospital bed for *you*."

She finally agreed.

Kicking into hospital survival mode, I found a clean sink where I could brush my teeth, scored a pair of comfortable scrubs from the nurses, and settled into a vinyl covered chair by my dad's bedside. As he slept calmly, I pulled out my Bible and began to read. I read a few scriptures that I had underlined, and then I prayed for a while. When I ran across a verse that had ministered to me in the past, I praised God with singing under my breath. Since it was clear sleep wasn't on the horizon, I sat surrendered in the Lord's presence for hours. When

I finished, I felt so full of the Holy Spirit that I had to be floating above my chair.

Just then my dad stirred. "Do you need something?" I asked quietly.

His eyes were half open and he was still groggy, but he began to talk. "I haven't always done what I should have," he confessed. My dad hadn't committed his life to Christ until he was in his fifties. With the threat of cancer hanging over his head, he was taking that commitment seriously.

I felt like the five-year-old little girl who needed to say something nice to my daddy so he wouldn't leave. But the peace of the Lord's presence strengthened me.

"Daddy," I told him, "when we confess our sins to God, he forgives us and cleanses us from all unrighteousness. We confess, and God takes care of the rest." (I had just read 1 John 1:9.)

"But I have to pay for my sins," he protested.

"Daddy, Jesus already did. Nothing we do can ever match the price he paid for us on the cross."

"You're smart," my dad said with a slight smile. Then he drifted back to sleep and the moment was gone.

I don't know if my words helped him that morning, but they sure helped me. The time I spent in the Lord's presence had prepared my heart for healing. I went from feeling like a timid little girl to a confident woman who knew she would never be without her heavenly Father.

Polish Your Jewels

- Do you have a hard time slowing down? If you're a driven person, you may have to make an appointment with yourself!

- Carve out that time and simply sit in the Lord's presence. Open his Word, pray, sing his praises, or just sit quietly so that the Lord has time to heal your heart and make you whole.

Day 19: Clean Slate

Have mercy on me, O God,
    according to your unfailing love;
according to your great compassion
    blot out my transgressions.
Wash away all my iniquity
    and cleanse me from my sin.
Surely you desire truth in the inner parts;
    you teach me wisdom in the inmost place.
Cleanse me with hyssop, and I will be clean;
    wash me, and I will be whiter than snow.
Create in me a pure heart, O God,
    and renew a steadfast spirit within me.
Do not cast me from your presence
    or take your Holy Spirit from me.
Restore to me the joy of your salvation
    and grant me a willing spirit, to sustain me.

(Psalm 51:1–2, 6–7, 10–12)

....

Scripture Insight: Keeping a clean slate of your heart and mind is easier said than done. It's easy to let resentment toward others build up when you have been treated unfairly. But in recovery meetings, I've heard wise people say, "Resentment is my drinking poison and hoping you die!" They also warn that "resentment does more to harm the vessel in which it's stored than the object on which it's poured." My friend Daniel understood that, which is why he took the high road when Charlie didn't deserve it.

Lost and Found

Daniel was a born leader, so when his senior class was assigned a challenging project to be completed before graduation, they immediately voted him their chairperson. They had to create a treatment program for some hard-core kids in the community. They didn't just have to write a paper about what they would do, like they had in earlier classes; they actually had to facilitate a program—choose a therapy, interview counselors, figure out finances, and be ready to implement it. Many projects that senior students prepared would end up as viable treatment programs for the community. But if your class project was poorly conceived or prepared, you might not get your degree.

Thank God for Daniel. His dad was a local pastor with a lot of experience in administration. Daniel was capable and fair, and everyone appreciated him—everyone except Charlie. From the beginning, it seemed that Charlie challenged Daniel's every word.

At first, Charlie picked on his ideas. Then he began to criticize him personally. "Nice tie," he remarked as a meeting was getting underway. "Did your mommy buy that for you?" Daniel refused to be riled by Charlie's juvenile remarks, but he had to ask God's help to keep from resenting his rival. It was a constant process because Charlie hardly ever let up.

Finally, the women on the committee had enough, so they approached Daniel. "We think you need to confront him," Lisa offered.

"We value all of your ideas," Jennifer added, "and we know we couldn't do this without you. It's difficult to see Charlie try to erode your leadership nearly every time we get together."

"Thanks for watching my back," Daniel answered, "but I think I understand what's going on. He's told us that his dad was a drug addict who didn't help him at all with his schooling. He probably thinks I had it too easy."

"You're capable *and* kind," Lisa retorted. "No wonder Charlie is jealous of you."

"As the group leader, I am responsible to all of you. That means I need to talk to Charlie so that you can feel more comfortable in our meetings. Please pray for me and for Charlie, and I'll do it as soon as possible."

Daniel asked to meet with Charlie over coffee. With all the tact he could muster, he approached his classmate about the constant criticism. He didn't accuse or try to psychoanalyze, he just asked if they could talk about some of Charlie's negative remarks.

Charlie denied everything, even the cutting comments that everyone in the group had heard him say. He depicted Daniel as an insecure guy who was jealous of him. After several skilled tries at presenting the truth, Daniel said to himself, *I gave it my best shot. Now I have to shake the dust off my feet and keep walking* (see Mark 6:11).

Daniel delicately shared his experience with the group, being careful not to run Charlie into the ground. *I have to keep my side of the street clean,* Daniel thought, *despite what Charlie does.*

Not long after the fruitless coffee shop encounter, Charlie showed up to meet with the group looking clearly bedraggled. "Are you okay?" Lisa asked, more out of curiosity than concern.

"My dad's in the hospital, and it's not looking good."

"Then what are you doing here?" Lisa said.

"My car's in the shop and I can't afford to fly."

"You can take my car," Daniel offered without hesitation. "I just filled it with gas. Here are the keys."

Charlie sat motionless for several seconds before he spoke. "Thanks, man," he sheepishly responded. "Are you sure?"

"You need to see your dad. Of course, I'm sure."

Daniel confided later that "it was supernatural response. The natural me would have said, 'No way am I going to help that guy. He doesn't deserve it.' Something changed in me in that moment. I lost a load of useless resentment. God took it away. I found the true peace that comes from following God in obedience—even if it's difficult."

Polish Your Jewels

- Read Psalm 51:6, "Surely you desire truth in the inner parts; you teach me wisdom in the inmost place." Take inventory right now of any resentment you may be holding on to. Ask the Lord to show you the truth.

- Read Psalm 51:10, "Create in me a pure heart, O God, and renew a steadfast spirit within me." Confess that unforgiving attitude to the Lord.

- Read Matthew 18: 21–22, "Then Peter came to Jesus and asked, 'Lord, how many times shall I forgive my brother when he sins against me? Up to seven times?' Jesus answered, 'I tell you, not seven times, but seventy-seven times.'" This means we may have to continue forgiving the hurt until our resentment is gone. Ask the Lord to make you willing to do that.

Day 20: Exempt

I said, "Oh, that I had the wings of a dove!
   I would fly away and be at rest." (Psalm 55:6)

....

Scripture Insight: We live in a culture that worships productivity. Some other cultures have siestas each day, a time when they close up shop and rest. Still others pause from the daily grind to share tea. Not we Americans! We slam coffee and keep on going until we drop and then castigate others for being lazy. "We have to keep up with the Joneses. It's a dog-eat-dog world," we've been warned. But God counsels us not to run with the dogs—rest. That is easier said than done.

Have you ever wanted to fly away from your daily cares and rest? I learned a beautiful lesson about slowing down, but as is often the case with me, I learned it the hard way.

Mommy Dragon

I'm not one of those people for whom the idea of rest comes easily. I struggle with slowing down. I have a relentless agenda of things that need to get done, even though my soul loves the benefit of rest.

During my school years, I had to pull a 4.0 grade point average, be president of every club, and struggle for first chair in band. Whether it was my weight, grades, housekeeping, or parenting, I made myself neurotic trying to prove that I was an achiever.

One day in my late twenties—after chasing two preschoolers all day, cleaning up the same mess again and again, and wondering why I had agreed not only to lead a Bible study group but to host it as well—I collapsed in a heap of exhaustion. As I sat in my sorry state of self-loathing, the words of Christ echoed in my head: "Come to me, all you who are weary and burdened, and I will give you rest."

Feeling guilty and discouraged for yelling at my kids, I picked up my Bible to read the passage that was echoing in my head from Matthew 11:28–30, "Come to me, all you who are weary and burdened, and I will give you rest. Take my yoke upon you and learn from me, for I am gentle and humble in heart, and you will find rest for your souls. For my yoke is easy and my burden is light."

God showed me in that moment that I am not a human doing; I get to be a human being. What a relief! Having grown up in a household where love had to be earned, I filled my days with endless striving toward the obscure goal of being loveable. In the midst of my mommy meltdown, God let me know that he loved me in spite of myself.

I decided to look up the word rest in Strong's Concordance, where I discovered that the New Testament word for *rest* literally meant "exempt." I heard the Lord say, "You're exempt from striving, Linda. You're enough." I had spent so much time trying to prove that I was lovable.

Then in one amazing God moment, the Lord showed me that he loved me, even at my worst.

I continued to read from Matthew 11: "Take my yoke upon you and learn from me for I am gentle and humble in heart." When I'm in my hyper-vigilant overachiever mode, I am anything but gentle and humble! I'm harried, angry, and impatient. Everyone around me could attest to that. Just ask my poor children, who were cowering in their rooms that day, fearing that the mommy dragon would breathe fire again.

Mommy dragons can fly. So can Superwoman, but I didn't have to be either. Sitting I could fly away to find rest in God's unconditional love and healing for my broken soul.

Polish Your Jewels

- In Matthew 11:29–30, Christ's "yoke" refers to his instructions for our lives. How does Christ's instructions for living differ from yours?

- Write out what keeps you from resting. Is it a need for approval or a fear of letting someone down? Is it drive to be good enough for God?

- Can you trade yokes with Christ and find rest? Give your burden over to the Lord So you can receive the peace he has for you.

Day 21: Casting

Cast your cares on the LORD
    and he will sustain you;
      he will never let the righteous fall. (Psalm 55:22)

....

Scripture Insight: I found a rich nugget of truth in this verse that brings me peace whenever I need it. It's the word *sustain*. Here's what it means in the Hebrew: "to provide," "to feed," "to guide," or "to comprehend." God understands why you feel the way you do. Did you ever just want somebody to understand your feelings? Your husband doesn't get you. Neither do your teenagers or your boss at work. But God gets you. He comprehends what's going on around you. You don't have to worry about tomorrow because he's already there.

That's not all. The Hebrew word translated as *sustain* also means "to nurture" and "to hold." Not only does God comprehend your hurt and understand your need, he will nurture and hold you. All this is implied by the Hebrew word *kuwl*. (In English it's pronounced "cool." I think it is pretty cool, don't you?)

The Sky Is Falling

I sat holding the receiver, too stunned to cry. "Lin, are you there?" my dad's voice asked.

"I'm here."

"The doctors are going to let me know my treatment plan by the end of this week. I wanted you to know."

"Please keep me in the loop," I said. "If they want to do surgery, I'll be on a plane right away."

"You don't have to do that for me."

"I have to do it for *me*," I explained.

I assured Dad that I would be praying for him and hung up the phone. My parent's time zone was three hours later than ours. Even though I really needed someone to share this with, I couldn't bring myself to wake my husband so early. Our church had just begun a building project. A lot of work was involved, and I didn't want to add this worry to the pile on his plate.

I decided to strap on my Adidas and go for a run. I found myself fretting with each footfall: *My dad has lost three siblings to cancer. Those aren't very good odds. All the years he spent smoking can't be good, either.* My thoughts rambled.

I ran through the front door no less stressed than when I left. As I lay on the floor to stretch out, I saw it—a huge dip in the entire living room ceiling. It shouldn't have come as such a surprise. We lived in an older manufactured home. It was pretty flimsy, and there was always something breaking. My kids often referred to it as our cardboard house.

"Bruce," I called out. "Honey, I think you need to see this."

He stumbled in and I pointed to the ceiling. "Let me get some coffee and I'll check it out," he assured me.

Before I left for work, Bruce made his way onto the roof to discover it was caving in. It would need immediate repairs and would cost who knew how much.

"Lord, I really don't need this right now," I prayed. I could hear my former pastor saying, "Worry is like a rocking chair. It gives you something to do, but you don't get anywhere!" I was wasting my time worrying, so I decided to give my troubles over to the Lord.

I pulled out a pad of paper and listed every detail I could think of about each issue: my dad's daunting diagnosis, this seemingly insurmountable building program, and the hassle of having a ceiling ready to fall in. When I finished my worry list, I scrawled a date by it and prayed to lay all of those troubles at the Lord's feet. Then I purposed in my heart not to pick them back up again. I headed into the day feeling prayed up and shored up.

The weeks ahead held a hospital visit to my dad, a fundraiser of epic proportions for our building project, and the upheaval of repairing the roof and ceiling of our house. Yet we all survived.

Several years passed and I was rereading my journal. When I saw the list I had made on that stressful morning,

I marveled. God had handled each of the problems I had *cast* on him in an amazing way. As I read that journal entry, I was standing in the church building that I was convinced we couldn't afford. My dad had sailed through his surgery and undergone several rounds of chemo with few ill effects. And the ceiling—wait until you hear about that!

Our neighbor was our insurance man. He called out a repairman who said that it looked like lightning had struck our roof. (I thanked God profusely that he had protected us from any harm. We were unaware it had even happened.) The repairman estimated that it would take at least $17,000 to repair all the damage. Our good neighbor and insurance man promptly issued us a check.

Then a roofer from our church surveyed the damage and said he could put things back together for only $7,000. We used the rest of the money as a down payment on a piece of property so we could build a new house, one that wasn't made out of cardboard! God really did sustain us. I can't tell you how *cool* that feels.

Polish Your Jewels

- Do the circumstances in your life seem intimidating and insurmountable?

- Write a list of your burdens in your journal and place a date next to your list. Leave room next to each item to record God's amazing answer to your concerns.

- Write down the definition for *sustain* and read it until it becomes part of your DNA and you can recall it when life is too much for you to handle.

Day 22: Refuge

My soul finds rest in God alone;
  my salvation comes from him.
He alone is my rock and my salvation;
  he is my fortress, I will never be shaken.
Find rest, O my soul, in God alone;
  my hope comes from him.
He alone is my rock and my salvation;
  he is my fortress, I will not be shaken.
My salvation and my honor depend on God;
  he is my mighty rock, my refuge.
Trust in him at all times, O people;
  pour out your hearts to him,
  for God is our refuge. (Psalm 62:1–2, 5–8)

....

Scripture Insight: When life dishes up more than I can put on my plate, I often recite the words in these verses: God is "my rock and my salvation." He's my "fortress." I need a fortress to shelter me from the stress life brings. I don't have the words this side of heaven to thank God for how he has proven to me again and again that he is my mighty rock and my refuge.

God's Tapestry

When the pastoral search committee issued a formal invitation to hire my husband, Bruce and I had some concerns. Don't get me wrong. Everything about the church in Oakhurst, from the friendly people to the surrounding Sierra Mountains, seemed perfect. But our youngest daughter had challenging heart problems, so we weren't sure she would thrive at the higher elevation. We made an appointment to see her doctor.

Dr. Jue had been Ashley's cardiologist for three years, and he loved her as much as we loved him. We explained our possible plans as he examined Ashley.

"She seems to be pretty strong right now. We are a few years out from another surgery. You could give it a try and see how she does at that elevation," he mused.

"In other words, we need to rent, not buy," Bruce off-commented.

"Yes," Dr. Jue responded. Then he remarked, "Wait a minute." He held up his finger and hurried out of the room. He returned as quickly as he left, holding an 8 x 10 glossy of a gorgeous house. Laying it in front of us, he offered, "This belongs to a colleague of mine at USC Medical Center. It's in Oakhurst, and he's asked me to keep a lookout for possible renters. The house has two thousand square feet with a trout pond in the front yard and a seventy-five-foot waterfall that pours right into the Fresno River in back."

"That's an amazing place," Bruce said. "He probably figured you could find a doctor to rent it. I'm afraid the housing allowance for a pastor wouldn't come close to paying for a place like this."

"I wouldn't be so sure," Dr. Jue responded. "I've known your family for three years. I'll put in a good word for you with Dr. Takahashi. He's looking for responsible renters, and I think he would be hard pressed to do better than you."

We thanked the good doctor for his kindness and vote of confidence, but inside we both felt the house was way out of our league. We pretty much dismissed it as an option—until that evening.

The phone rang about 9:00 and a soft-spoken man introduced himself as Mike Takahashi. He explained that Dr. Jue had highly recommended us as renters, so he and his wife Marcia wanted to meet us the following Saturday. We agreed to meet, even though we assumed our meager housing allowance wasn't near the amount his fabulous home deserved.

We spent the day with the Takahashis and fell in love with them. They showed us their house. Our kids fed the trout and played in the river. We talked about the church they attended in LA and about the plans we had for the church we had been called to serve in Oakhurst.

At the end of the day, as we sat on the deck, Marcia stated, "We had a businessman from Sacramento express interest in renting the place. He offered us $1,400 a month, but I really want to rent this house to a family. There's so much for kids to enjoy here. I would like to see your family here. Are you interested?"

"Who wouldn't be?" Bruce replied. "But the housing allowance the church will be giving us is only $750 a month. We know you can get much more than that."

"Can we have a minute?" she asked. She and Mike disappeared into the house. In a few minutes, they emerged, smiling ear to ear. "We'll take $750 with one request. We would like to be able to stay here with you on some weekends when we can get away from LA."

"That would be great for us," I responded. "You get to enjoy your house and we would love to spend time with you!"

That was the beginning of a delightful friendship. We shared many dinners with the Takahashis, enjoying the mountains and each other's company.

While we were there, it became clear that Ashley needed another heart surgery. There was doubt as to whether the surgeons at our local children's hospital could handle it, with all the complexity of her multiple diagnoses. Bruce called Mike for a listening ear and got so much more.

"Dr. Jue sent me Ashley's file, and her situation is unique and complicated. There are probably only two places in the world that could handle a surgery of this magnitude.

One is in Minnesota and the other is UCLA. Both are practically impossible to get into, but you happen to know someone with influence. Hillel Laks at UCLA owes me a favor. He can return that favor by performing Ashley's surgery. Having studied under Christian Barnard,[1] Laks is the most prominent heart surgeon in the world right now."

Fighting back tears, Bruce could hardly respond. "How can I ever thank you?"

"Seeing Ashley thrive will be thanks enough," Mike responded.

After a few stressful weeks of waiting, we had a surgery date with the renowned Dr. Hillel Laks. With the amazing surgeon's skill and a ton of people praying, Ashley sailed through her surgery. As we visited her in cardiac recovery, an adorable little nurse trained at UCLA commented, "This is, like, a miracle and stuff. Ashley is, like, getting better by the minute!"

We didn't truly grasp the magnitude of the miracle until a few days later. As Ashley was recovering, Bruce went down to the medical center bookstore at UCLA. My husband is an avid reader, so he decided to reduce his stress by reading some medical journals.

Bruce picked up a surgeon's journal published several years earlier. He read that the procedure used to repair Ashley's set of congenital heart problems had been performed 347 times and had never succeeded. Bruce later

---

1. South African cardiac surgeon Christian Barnard performed the world's first successful human-to-human heart transplant.

asked Mike if the surgical procedure had been updated. He said no. The only difference between past surgeries and Ashley's was the precision of the surgeon, and she had been blessed with the best in the world.

If I live to be a hundred, I will continue to be awed by the amazing tapestry God put together on our behalf. If the church hadn't called us to be their pastors, we would not have needed to visit Dr. Jue. Then we would not have needed a house to rent in Oakhurst. We would not have met Mike Takahashi, who introduced us to one of only two doctors in the world who could perform the surgery to save her life. I believe God still works miracles today!

Polish Your Jewels

- What difficult situations have you quaking in fear today? Know that God is weaving an intricate tapestry to take care of you.

- Look back at how God has dealt with you in the past. Think of all the prayers he has answered up to now.

- Celebrate the way you have come through seemingly impossible situations before and don't panic in the face of today's.

Day 23: My Song

God sets the lonely in families,
    he leads forth the prisoners with singing.

(Psalm 68:6)

....

Scripture Insight: Another word for *psalm* is *song*. Zephaniah 3:17 says, "He (the LORD) will rejoice over you with singing." When I looked through the Psalms to find my song, I found it in this verse. God truly placed my lonely heart in a family of believers who loved me, warts and all. He freed me from the prison of sin and shame, and that's worth singing about!

Gilligan's Island

The South usually conjures up visions of front porch swings, magnolia blossoms, and the faint scent of wisteria. For me it's memories of rage, abandonment, violence, and the smell of stale cigarette smoke. I was a kid from a broken home who always felt like I was on the outside of life looking in.

When my mom wasn't working at the diner, she was either yelling at us kids or sleeping. Depressed people do that.

Mama's punishments never fit the crimes. It was crazy making. You could hurl obscenities at the neighbors at the top of your lungs in the morning and that would go unpunished, but if you spilled your milk at the table that night, you could be beaten until your face swelled shut. It was easy to see why my dad left. I wanted to go too, but I was just a kid.

I liked school, and I wasn't a bad student, but I figured, "Why try?" I was stuck going nowhere, just like my mom. She often told us that if she didn't have us kids, she could have done something with her life. Without realizing it, I caught a bad case of "What's the use?" So I didn't apply myself to my studies.

I preferred instead to watch *Gilligan's Island* on television. I think I identified with him—forever trapped on a deserted island and hopeless in his efforts to leave.

Then God showed up in the form of our neighbor from across the street, Maude Gober, who invited our family to church. Most of the folks in the neighborhood thought we were the divorced family that ought to be avoided, but Mrs. Gober knew Jesus could make a difference.

My mom didn't go to church. She sent the kids. Perhaps Mama thought she would wreak retribution on those "holy-rollin' hypocrites," as she was fond of calling them, by sending her reprobate kids to church. But they didn't treat me like a bother; they treated me like a blessing.

Because of their concern for me, I gave my heart to Jesus one Sunday in June. Weeping at the altar, I felt loved for the very first time in my life.

The folks in that church wrapped their arms around me and became my family. A retired pastor there bought me my first leather bound Bible with my name imprinted on the front. My Sunday school teacher made sure I got to church when Mrs. Gober couldn't take me. If she weren't available, Richard the youth pastor gave me a ride on the church bus. I would plant myself behind him and pummel him with questions about God, which he would answer with the patience of Job, no matter how lame they were.

He answered everyone's questions at youth group meetings on Thursday, the same night as *Gilligan's Island*. Now I had much more to live for than a television show, so I was at youth group meetings, riveted to Richard's wise words. I had hope, direction, and a purpose. My church family believed in me, and that helped me believe in myself.

I got serious about my schoolwork. Now I wanted to do something with my life—something for God. When it came time for me to go to college, the pastor of the church made sure I got there.

I don't know if "it takes a village to raise a child," but that little country church in the buckle of the Bible Belt helped to raise this one. The Lord placed my lonely heart in a new family and released me from my prison of dysfunction with a new song to sing.

Polish Your Jewels

- Sit down with a cup of tea, a notepad, and a couple of hours stretched in front of you. Open your Bible to the Psalms and prayerfully ask God to show you your song. Maybe you will find several.

- Read Zephaniah 3:17, "The LORD your God is with you, he is mighty to save. He will take great delight in you, he will quiet you with his love, he will rejoice over you with singing."

- When you read "your psalm," understand it in the light of this verse in Zephaniah. Recognize how much God delights in you.

Day 24: Rewards

For the LORD God is our sun and our shield.
  He gives us grace and glory.
The LORD will withhold no good thing
  from those who do what is right.
O LORD of Heaven's Armies,
  what joy for those who trust in you.

(Psalm 84:11–12 NLT)

....

Scripture Insight: Have you ever found yourself frustrated when God doesn't answer a request in the way you thought he should? What a question! Of course, you have! Many people distance themselves from the Lord when they don't understand his plan. Others give up on God altogether because they lack the patience to wait for him to fulfill his perfect purpose in their lives. Just because things aren't working out the way we planned, we shouldn't assume they aren't working out the way God planned.

Good Things

Gene was athletic, intelligent, and good-looking— and he wasn't vain about all he had going for him. He met Diane at Christian camp. She was the attractive, smart capable counterpart to all Gene had to offer. Everyone could see they were made for each other.

They were both college graduates who loved working with kids. Summer camp seemed like a great place to be before entering the work force and having to get a "real job," as Gene described it.

"I love being a camp counselor," he exclaimed. "Here kids can let go of the cares of the world and hear more clearly from God. I like being part of their 'aha moments.' It's such a rush seeing a hardcore kid get a clue."

Diane enjoyed being a camp counselor too. As challenging as it was, the couple maintained good boundaries and didn't let their relationship affect the important job of being there for God's kids.

At the time Gene and Diane were dating, Christians had not begun to think it was okay to sleep together before they were married. They obeyed God's Word and stayed chaste. That didn't stop them from getting closer. In fact, it made them closer because they spent time getting to know each other's hearts.

After summer, Gene was heading back east for an intern position at a parachurch organization that worked with street kids. Diane was going home to California to apply for her first full-time teaching position. A long-distance relationship would be a challenge, but their love could handle it.

After nearly nine months of daily phone calls and a few visits back and forth, Gene believed Diane was the girl for him. He proposed and they set a wedding date for six months out so Diane could plan the ceremony she had always dreamed of.

Ministering to street kids was demanding, but Gene never let himself get too scheduled to spend time with God. "I don't want to be so busy with the work of the Lord that I forget the Lord of the work," Gene said. He would carve out time every day to get on his knees. One evening, not long after he visited Diane, he felt a nudge from the Lord to break off the engagement with Diane. He felt no fear about the marriage, but he had a definite impression that the Lord was telling him to stop.

"I was scheduled to see her in three weeks, so I stayed on my knees practically the entire time," Gene recalls. "Nothing changed; that feeling remained. I called Diane with a heavy heart, but I didn't share with her what was on it. I told her I wanted to take her to dinner at a swanky place I knew she enjoyed.

"That evening, Diane showed up for dinner as beautiful as ever. We had an awesome time talking and laughing together. Just as the waitress was bringing dessert, Diane said, 'I'm so glad you booked this place so we could talk. I want to share with you how God has been speaking to me in prayer.'"

Diane then told Gene that she believed the Lord did not want them to marry. She said she still felt drawn to him, "but the more I pray, the more God makes that message clear."

Gene confirmed this by sharing what God had revealed to him during his prayer times. "After finishing our dessert, we went walking on the beach," Gene says. "Hand in hand, we laughed, cried, and said our good-byes.

"As I boarded the plane to head home, I fought back tears. *I was obedient to your will, Lord, so why don't I feel good right now? I miss Diane already,* I protested. Right away, this verse flooded onto my head from Psalm 84:11: 'For the LORD God is our sun and our shield. He gives us grace and glory. The Lord will withhold no good thing from those who do what is right.' An immediate peace calmed my soul, as I heard the Lord whisper, *As good as Diane is, I have someone better for you.* In that moment, I decided to trust God's plan for me.

"Today," Gene shared with a group of us, "I am married to Joanna. There is no doubt that she is the girl for me. I can't imagine my life without her. There were some lonely times after Diane and I went our separate ways, but what Joanna and I have was worth waiting for."

I heard Gene tell that story in front of hundreds of angst-ridden adolescents at a large gathering of Christian young people thirty-five years ago. His story made such an impact on me that I never forgot it. I reflected on it when I was walking on the winding road of relationships looking for true love in my own life. I pondered that verse from Psalms so many times when God didn't do things the way I thought he should. After all these years, I am convinced they are true. If God doesn't give me what I want, it's because he has something better, and as the verse reminds me, "Happy am *I* when I trust in him."

Polish Your Jewels

- Have you ever experienced a battle of the wills with God? Who won?

- Is it possible to do what is right and not feel good about it right away, especially when you have to give up something you want?

- Journal about a time you obeyed God in spite of your feelings. How has he rewarded you for following him?

Day 25: Safety

He will order his angels
     to protect you wherever you go. (Psalm 91:11 NLT)

....

Scripture Insight: I have always been fascinated by stories about angels. While I collected every story I could find about these benevolent beings, I never knew anyone personally who had experienced an angel encounter—until my daughter told me this story. I don't know whether a true angel showed up to help her or some kind man demonstrated angelic kindness, but I am one mother who will be forever grateful.

Ashley's Angel

When my daughter turned nineteen, she announced that she was moving from our small mountain town in central California to Pasadena. I wasn't crazy about my younger daughter moving to the big city, but I remembered the Beach Boys song, "The Little Old Lady from Pasadena." If my daughter was determined to relocate to southern California, I supposed that Pasadena was a safer choice than most.

After a couple of years of junior college, she and her roommate Laura decided to transfer to the university. That meant moving away from the little old ladies in Pasadena and settling for a place that was less advantageous, to say the least.

"We're not living in the ghetto. We're just living in the 'ghett,'" Ashley joked, trying to reassure her parents she would be safe. She was right. It wasn't completely frightening, but there were enough shady characters and siren sounds to keep a mother on her knees every night asking God to send angels to watch over her petite blonde beauty living in Los Angeles.

After parking her car one night, Ashley cautiously began walking to her door. She passed a group of guys who took notice of the fact she was alone. She and Laura had a habit of calling each other as soon as they got out of the car and staying on the cell phone until they were safely inside, but tonight Laura wasn't home either. Pretending to be on the phone, Ashley heard footsteps following her. With her heart in her throat, she breathed a prayer for safety.

Then she heard a voice behind her, "Sweetie, you're being followed. I am just going to walk with you until you get to your door."

"Normally, if some guy calls me 'Sweetie,' he's the one I want to avoid," Ashley said. "But the minute this stranger opened his mouth, I felt safe.

"He didn't actually walk with me. He stayed a few steps behind me. I reached my apartment, put my key in the door, and turned to thank him, but he was gone. He was nowhere in sight."

Ashley didn't get to express her gratitude to her benefactor that night, but I haven't stopped thanking God for answering this fretting mother's prayers.

Polish Your Jewels

- Have you ever experienced someone's kindness that was practically angelic in how it ministered to you at the time?

- How can you demonstrate angelic care for someone in your world this week?

- How do you feel when you rely on the Holy Spirit's power in you to make that happen?

Day 26: Turning Loose

But the love of the Lord remains forever
    with those who fear him.
His salvation extends to the children's children
    of those who are faithful to his covenant,
    of those who obey his commandments!

                    (Psalm 103:17–18 NLT)

Scripture Insight: "Your children are not your children; they are the sons and daughters of life's longing for itself." I read this in Kahlil Gibran's *The Prophet* my senior year of college.

Now fast-forward a few decades. I was the parent, who realized I had to open my hand and let my girl go, but I had the assurance the Lord never would.

Push Me Higher, Mommy

My daughter Sarah was born brave. As the oldest of my three kids, she definitely fit the characteristics that psychologists have observed about the oldest child in a family's birth order. A natural high-achiever, she first learned to talk in full sentences. Within a week of her first step, she was running to meet her dad as he walked through the door each evening. The second I set her on a swing set, she shouted, "Push me higher, Mommy. Now turn loose." So why should I have been surprised when she told me she was considering enlistment in the military?

At twenty-eight years old, in the middle of her doctoral studies in psychology, Sarah decided that she wanted to help soldiers returning from Iraq with post-traumatic stress disorder. Her husband Shaun was all for it. Shaun had served two terms in Iraq just before he became an EMT. He was even considering reenlisting to join his wife in the air force. *I'm glad he's supportive,* I thought, *but I'm not convinced that my daughter should be in the military while our country is at war.*

I did my best to form my worries into prayers as I considered my daughter's desire. I wondered where she might be stationed. She assured us that her work would keep her out of harm's way, but I knew our daughter. She had wanted to drive four hours from work to the coast to meet us on our vacation only a month after she got her driver's license! I worried she would volunteer for hazardous duty. I was concerned about *her* stress level while she treated post-traumatic stress in others. I hadn't shared these concerns with her because I didn't want to be a meddling mother. If she believed the Lord was calling her to help soldiers, who was I to get in her way?

Sarah kept us informed as she received a scholarship in the field of neuro-psychology at one of three air force bases in the United States. She kept us in the loop as she traveled to interview at each base. When she accepted a residency fourteen hundred miles away, I sat aside my mother's sadness to rejoice with her at this prestigious placement. The week before she left, we met at Time for Tea, a darling teahouse in our little town. Sarah and I had enjoyed tea together since she was barely old enough to hold a teacup. We could always talk more easily over tea.

As we sat across from each other with our salad and scones in the Alice in Wonderland room, what we didn't say was even more important than what we did.

I said, "How's your salad?" I didn't say, "I will miss your living just down the road from me."

Sarah said, "My salad's great. I love the dressing." She didn't say, "I'm scared. I've been academic for so long I've forgotten how to be physical. I don't want to be the weakest link at boot camp."

I said, "I hear the base is beautiful." I didn't say, "I'm worried about your having so much stress so far from home—without me, I mean."

Sarah said, "I've met several officers who came back to retire near the base because they loved the area so much." She didn't say, "Shaun and I are finally ready to have kids and it will be hard, living fourteen hundred miles away from my mom."

So it went, back and forth, text and subtext. Sarah's words were meant to reassure her fretful mother. But what I really heard was, "Push me higher, Mommy. Now turn loose." So I did.

"For their souls dwell in the house of tomorrow, which you cannot visit," Gibran wrote, "not even in your dreams."

Polish Your Jewels

- Have you ever had trouble letting go of your possessions, house, children, addictions, or health?

- Post Psalm 103:1–15 on your computer screen-saver, refrigerator, or mirror. Read it often as you practice "letting go and letting God."

- Use it as self-talk to help you release the fear that keeps you clinging to your stuff or wringing your hands in wasted worry.

Day 27: Illumination

Your word is a lamp to my feet
and a light for my path. (Psalm 119:105)

....

Scripture Insight: Do you find that you can read the Bible over and over and get something new out of it each time? God's Word is alive. It tells us that his mercies are new every morning; those mercies are revealed to us as we read his Word.

In its pages, I have discovered how to parent my children and how to keep my marriage alive. I've found instructions to maintain a healthy work ethic and how to be a leader worth following. But most of all, I have found a light of hope on the dark nights when my soul really needs it.

Love Notes From God

At a women's retreat, the leader placed tiny manila envelopes on our chairs and let each woman open it to find a verse that God chose specifically for her. The verses seemed tailor-made for each lady, as if God was personally speaking to each one of us. My next conference was two months away, and I couldn't wait to use the same idea to help the ladies realize God's generous love.

I poured over the Bible and prayerfully selected around thirty different scriptures. I wrote down the reference of each verse and emailed them to a friend who figured out how to print each verse on card stock. We placed them in the tiny envelopes, and I continued to pray that each verse would find its way to the right needy heart.

During the next retreat, I spoke about how much God loves us. During a sharing time, these precious women told about some of their struggles. Jennifer, in her early forties, said that her husband had left her for a younger woman, and she was faced with figuring out finances for the first time in twenty years.

Amber had just lost her mother and felt frustrated at how debilitated this loss made her feel. "I know everyone goes through this. I didn't expect my mom to live forever, but I didn't expect to lose her quite this soon," she confessed.

Irene, an elegant lady in her early sixties, expressed her insecurity at rejoining the job market. However, her current financial condition necessitated it.

I placed a chair in the middle of the room. One by one, we all prayed earnestly for each lady who was willing to share her burden with the group.

The next morning as each woman walked in, there was a tiny envelope with *her* verse in it waiting on each chair. When I reached the appropriate point in my talk, I asked if any of them would like to share her scripture with the group.

Jennifer read Philippians 4:19 as she fought back tears. "And my God will meet all your needs according to his glorious riches in Christ Jesus." Of all the scriptures, God gave this one to the mom struggling to pay her bills.

Amber opened hers to find Psalm 55:22: "Cast your cares on the Lord and he will sustain you; he will never let the righteous fall." The day prior I had explained the meaning of the word *sustain*—to lead, guide, comprehend, nurture, and uphold. As she read her verse, Amber said that she knew the Lord understood her pain and he would get her through.

Irene read Isaiah 41:10: "So do not fear, for I am with you; do not be dismayed, for I am your God. I will strengthen you and help you; I will uphold you with my righteous right hand." We all cried as we realized how perfect these words were for Irene's current struggle. God's Word does not return void. That Sunday afternoon God proved his faithfulness to all of us present.

As I cleaned up and packed to go, I picked up a tiny envelope that rested on my seat. I opened it and read Isaiah 40:11: "He tends his flock like a shepherd: He gathers the lambs in his arms and carries them close to his heart; he gently leads those that have young." I wept quietly all the way home. When I gave the reference for this verse to my friend to print, I didn't include the last line: "He gently leads those who have young." In fact, it had been so long since I'd read this verse in its entirety, I had forgotten about this promise. However, I had been berating myself over the job I was doing as a parent.

I fretted about the time I spent in ministry, feeling guilty for not spending enough time with my kids, worrying that I would do irreparable damage to my precious children. In an amazing God-moment, the Lord showed me that he would gently and patiently lead this weary mother. What a gift this verse was to me that day! And what a love letter his Word is to us every day.

Polish Your Jewels

- What lessons for life have you learned from God's Word?

- Find a translation of the Bible you like and devote some time each day to reading it. If you miss a day because of your busy schedule, skip the guilt and shame of "missing your quiet time." Simply pick up your Bible the next day and read where you left off.

- Ask God to help you learn one meaningful verse a month for the rest of the year.

Day 28: Peace

You are my refuge and my shield;
    I have put my hope in your word.
Away from me, you evildoers,
    that I may keep the commands of my God!
Sustain me according to your promise, and I will live;
    do not let my hopes be dashed.

(Psalm 119:114-116)

....

Scripture Insight: Growing up in a dysfunctional home, my "truster" was busted. The world didn't feel like a safe place.

Then I met Jesus. He became my refuge and my shield. I put my hope in him and he restored my ability to trust others. He did not let my dreams of having a happy family be dashed.

You'll Be All Right

As soon as my son Jake learned to play guitar, we knew he had great promise as a musician. After high school, he moved to LA, worked hard waiting tables to pay the rent, and spent the rest of his time writing songs and looking for places to sing them. After a few years of playing gigs here and there, dealing with broken promises, and listening to promoters who were all wind-up and no pitch, he needed to come home and regroup.

Jake had a construction job that required him to get up in the wee hours of the morning. As he headed for a job site before dawn one day, words of assurance began to resonate in his head. Jake is a talented musician, so these words formed themselves into a melody. When he returned from work that evening, he said, "I got a song today and I really believe it's from God. It's his words speaking to me. Want to hear it?" With guitar in hand, Jake sang this heartfelt ballad:

I'm on the lonely road that you seek
When others say you are in too deep,
Oh, my dear child, now don't you weep…

I'm in the tree by your window,
And when you find yourself caught up hard in
 the throes
Of a wild, wicked world spinning out of control,
Just tap upon the glass and I'll be by your side in
 a flash.
I'll be by your side in a flash.

It's all right if you're scared. It's not your fault.
If you feel unprepared, I'll break your fall…

I know you're all right; it's the night that
 surrounds you.

It's the unknown that chills your bones and
   confounds you.
I know you're all right. I know you're all right.[1]

He made the song available via iTunes and his MySpace
page, and it inspired others. He received a call that one
of his high school buddies named Jon had been killed
in a car accident. His grief-stricken parents checked Jon's
MySpace page and found that just two nights before he
died, Jon was playing Jake's song and commenting about
how much he liked it. Jon's dad asked Jake if he would
sing it at his son's funeral.

Jake sang "You'll Be All Right" from his heart at the
service. He sang it for Jon's parents, his sisters, and especially
for Jon himself, whom I believe was tapping his toes on
streets of gold and saying, "I know. Oh, how I know!"

Polish Your Jewels

- Do you have dreams that seem impossible?

- Do you spend time in prayer about your dreams
  daily?

- Do you recognize that God is using you in spite
  of your apparent failures?

- Thank him for using you to bring his light to
  others.

---

1. Jake Newton, "You'll Be All Right." Used by permission.

Day 29: Online Encouragement

For the LORD will vindicate his people and have
compassion on his servants. (Psalm 135:14)

Scripture Insight: Have you ever been in a situation where
everything that you did seemed to turn out wrong? You
continue to put your best foot forward, only to feel it being
stepped on. Forty years of walking with God have taught
me that God's opinion is all that matters in the end anyway.

He Knows What We Need

After traveling fourteen hundred miles in a Prius
with four cats, her husband following behind in
his Jeep with the two dogs, my daughter Sarah
shoved everything into her Ohio home just in time to hop
a plane for Alabama to attend boot camp.

"It's officially called C.O.T., Comissioned Officer
Training," she informed me. "But it seems to me that if
your mealtime is reduced to ten minutes, your sleep to four
hours, and someone is constantly screaming two inches
from your face, it's boot camp!"

After four strenuous weeks there, she returned to Ohio
to report for duty at the base hospital in Dayton. As a
psychologist, she would be dealing with patients in the
mental health rotation.

"My caseload is a difficult one," she confided. "Soldiers returning from war and their families need all of the skill and attention I can muster. I keep wondering if I made the right choice to take this residency and finish my doctorate in the military."

I listened patiently to my daughter, knowing that exhaustion and stress from the last few weeks had finally caught up with her. I assured her that she would succeed as she always did, and I let her know I would be praying that God would give her the encouragement she needed.

As soon as I finished praying that day, I opened my e-mail. To my delight there was a note from a student I hadn't seen in ten years. I quickly forwarded Jeanna's email to Sarah, and we both cried. Here is what it said:

Hey, girl! It's Jeanna, I keep wanting to say, "Mrs. Newton" and I'm thirty years old. It's sad, I know! You are not going to believe this! It must be a God-thing, but I have been thinking about you and Sarah a lot in the last week, and I had no way of getting a hold of anyone....

I want you to know that you and your family got me though some really hard times in my life....

I remember one time in particular: I woke up with hives all over my face so, of course, I kept covering it with make up, which only made it worse and painful. I was reading to Sarah that day during recess in the back of the classroom, and she could tell that I wasn't okay.

She asked, "What's wrong? You look kind of swollen." I turned away thinking that she was going to make fun of me, but she didn't. She washed my face while I cried. I thought I was so ugly without the make up. Sarah convinced me saying, "The heck with anyone who doesn't like you for you!"

When Jeanna did a Google search for Bruce and me, she found our Web page with a photo of Sarah at her C.O.T. graduation in Alabama. Jeanna was now living in Birmingham herself, along with her husband and two children. She asked how she could contact Sarah, because "you guys have impacted my life, and changed me for the better."

After reading what Jeanna had written, Sarah's e-mail response came quickly:

Jeanna's letter made me cry. I needed this right now! I needed a reminder of why I am doing what I do, and I need to stay true to who I am. I can't believe Jeanna found us! Thanks for forwarding her note. It gives me the encouragement to be myself.

Love,
Sarah

I clicked off my computer and thanked God for bringing Jeanna back into our lives and allowing us to encourage her at a pivotal point in her life. I thanked him for inspiring

Jeanna to write a letter that was exactly what Sarah and I needed at the time. Then I praised him because he always knows exactly what all of us need all the time!

Polish Your Jewels

- Who can you encourage today? Send them a letter or an e-mail to do that.

- Encourage yourself by determining to "play to an audience of One." If you please God, that's all that matters in the end.

Day 30: Strength

For you created my inmost being;
  you knit me together in my mother's womb.
I praise you because I am fearfully and wonderfully
  made;
  your works are wonderful,
  I know that full well.
My frame was not hidden from you
  when I was made in the secret place.
When I was woven together in the depths of the
  earth,
  your eyes saw my unformed body.
All the days ordained for me
  were written in your book
  before one of them came to be. (Psalm 139:13–16)

....

Scripture Insight: Did it ever occur to you that nothing ever occurs to God? That was a profound realization for me. This scripture informs us that God knew exactly what we would experience every day of our lives, even before we were born.

It also tells us that he knew exactly what he was doing when he created us. I can lament my weaknesses (and the older I get, the more I have), or I can rejoice that I am fearfully and wonderfully made. I learned that from my younger daughter.

Through the Eyes of God

Our youngest child, Ashley, lived a pretty challenging childhood. By the time she was six years old, she had already undergone three heart surgeries, with many more expected in her lifetime. Just after her first surgery, a helpful nurse walked me through the steps to care for my fragile post-operative newborn as I took her home. Then she sat down on the edge of Ashley's bed, looked me in the eye, and said, "You have to be very careful not to create a cardiac cripple." Her somber tone caught me off guard.

She explained, "You will want to hover over her and keep her from doing things because you are worried that she is too fragile."

"That's exactly what I plan to do!" I exclaimed. "I've just spent the last ten days watching this delicate baby cling to life. I have every intention of walking out of here and protecting her from anything and everything that might endanger her."

"I know," said the nurse. "I can see it in your face. But you have to let her regulate herself so she won't grow up weak and helpless. She'll know what her limits are. Let her govern her own activity. With all she has to deal with for the rest of her life, she needs to feel as strong as possible."

I took this wise woman's words to heart. Ashley *did* learn to regulate herself, but she was around me most of the time. I knew this challenge would be greater as she approached school age.

At age five we were visiting Grandma. The little girl who lived next door was an only child, and she looked forward to having kids to play with. The minute we pulled into the driveway, I heard Melissa calling Ashley's name. A steep hill stood between Ashley and her would-be playmate, so I started to explain to my frail daughter that the path was too steep for her. Then I caught myself. Instead, I watched Ashley get out of the car and start toward the house next door. Then she came back to where her dad was standing and yelled for Melissa to come to her. The good nurse was right. I could count on Ashley to determine what she could handle.

I lost count of the times over the next ten years that I had to bite my tongue to keep from doing for Ashley what she was capable of doing for herself. Then one day she brought home a CD she had picked up at a youth concert at church. After listening to a song in her room, she came out with tears in her eyes and asked, "Mom, have you heard these words?"

The song was about a little girl in the musician's church who was going deaf. The lyrics said, "Mom loves it when she sings…Mom loves it when she plays…Mom loves it when she prays." The writer had clearly captured the angst of a mother who had to see her child struggle. As Ashley played it for me, we both cried. I looked at her and said, "Tell me about it."

Without hesitation, Ashley put her hands on her hips and quipped, "What do you mean? I'm not handicapped!"

"Of, course you're not. Not you." I shrugged my shoulders.

As Ashley returned to her bedroom, I headed for my bedroom and got on my knees. I thanked God that after four life-threatening heart surgeries, an endless list of hospital stays, and not being able to run and play like the rest of her friends, Ashley refused to consider herself handicapped. As far as she was concerned, she was as fearfully and wonderfully made as the rest of us.

God knew what he was doing when he formed her, and her strength continues to inspire people to this day. I know she certainly inspires me.

Polish Your Jewels

- Thank God for how fearfully and wonderfully you are made.

- Praise God for today—the new day he has ordained for you. What can you do for him today?

Day 31: Legacy

Let this be written for a future generation,
   that a people not yet created may praise the
   LORD. (Psalm 102:18)

....

Scripture Insight: Have you ever thought of what you're doing that will live on after you? What investment have you made in eternity?

Many years ago, my youth pastor's wife gave me a card with a picture of Jesus on the front that read, "Only one life, will soon be past; only what's done for Christ will last." From the moment I read these words they became the purpose statement of my life.

A Soaking Wet Fleece

When my husband Bruce and I started serving at Sierra Pines Church, in our tiny mountain town in central California, there were only thirty-five people in attendance. We were meeting at a scenic campground, but it wasn't uncommon for weather to roll in and dump loads of snow, making it impossible for any of us to get to church on Sunday morning. That left us scrambling for a place to meet and calling everyone late on Saturday night to tell them where that was.

Once we met at the pizza parlor. The manager attended the church, and he fired up the ovens so we could stay warm. Another Sunday we met in a hotel room at the Days Inn. Folks spilled out the door into the parking lot and held up umbrellas to keep the snow from soaking them! After that, we tried the local movie theatre. (I remember teaching junior church under a marquee that read, "Terminator 2.")

Eventually, the church purchased a two-thousand-square-foot building. It was small but stationary, and seekers didn't have to wonder where we were if they wanted to come to church that week.

We soon filled that little building. One service went to two, then three. After five services on Easter Sunday, we decided we needed to build a place that could house everyone in our church family. A generous gentleman in the fellowship offered a prime piece of property for a fraction of its market value because he believed in the changed lives he saw at church each week.

Despite such liberal support, building projects can breed fear in the hearts of churchgoers. That was true of Dave, who played on the worship team. He called the house one evening just after Bruce had presented his vision to the congregation and shared his skepticism. "I don't think I can support the direction you're going, Bruce. I've been around here for years, and everyone knows that the ridge where you want to build is dry as a bone. If you want to sustain a church with several hundred people, you have to have water, and I don't think this is the place to get it.

The man next door drilled eight hundred feet looking for water and got a dust bowl instead."

Bruce asked, "How many gallons per minute would a well have to produce to prove to you we're supposed to build on the land?"

"I have a number in mind," Dave said. "I've put a fleece before the Lord, and if we get a certain number of gallons per minute, I'll believe it's okay to build the church there. But I'm not going to tell you what that is."

Dave's doubts did not deter Bruce. The next day he and Ray, the church treasurer, drove to the property to meet with a well driller. Identifying a spot at the rear of the lot, John informed the men there was a good chance they would find about fifty to seventy-five gallons per minute if he drilled down 250 feet.

Then John climbed on a rig that looked like a huge flatbed truck with an enormous jackhammer attached to it. He fastened a twenty-foot section of pipe to the end of the device, turned on the deafening motor, and hammered into solid granite. John would drill down twenty feet, and then haul the pipe up and attach another twenty-foot section. Every foot of pipe cost the church ten dollars. This went on foot after foot, until finally at 320 feet John's rig struck water—but the flow registered only three gallons per minute, hardly enough to support the activities of several hundred people in and out on a weekly basis. On he drilled to 450 feet, where the rig registered ten more gallons a minute. Still that wasn't quite enough for the needs of a growing church. He attached another section of pipe and down went the drill.

By now, Ray was realizing the church owed John nearly five grand, and he was getting worried. As the church treasurer, that was his job.

"Does our contract give him permission to drill until he reaches a certain number of gallons per minute, or can we shut him down as we see fit?" Ray yelled to Bruce over the roar of the engine.

"I don't know. Let's go back to the office and see." They made the five-minute trip into town and found that the contract said they had the discretion to tell the driller to stop whenever they wanted. Upon returning, they found John was attaching pipe to reach 620 feet. Ray was just about to tell him to shut down when Bruce felt a nudge from God.

"Let him use one more section, Ray," Bruce urged. "If nothing happens, I'll pay for the extra twenty feet."

At that moment, John stood up on his rig and waved for the men to back up. A geyser of water erupted, drenching the rig and John, soaking the ground in a thirty-foot radius!

"There's your water," the drenched well-driller marveled with a grin.

"How many gallons per minute is it?" Bruce asked.

"I don't know. My equipment can't measure past one hundred. You have at least that. It's more than any well I've dug in this entire town!"

Bruce and Ray laughed until they nearly cried, rejoicing at the miracle God had prepared right in front of them.

"I can't wait to hear what Dave has to say about this," Ray remarked.

That evening, Bruce called his fearful friend. "Does one hundred gallons a minute get your fleece wet enough?" Bruce asked.

"You're lying," Dave accused. "This is some kind of joke."

"No, sir. I've got the report to prove it."

Bruce didn't need the report. Now the folks at Sierra Pines Church meet each week in a sixteen-thousand-square-feet facility, which we are quickly outgrowing. Who knows what God had planned for future generations?

Polish Your Jewels

- What are you investing that will live on after you?

- Bill Hybels is fond of saying, "The hope of the world is in the local church." Many ministries in the local church will make an investment in eternity. Ask God to show you where you can be of service to him. Commit to being part of his team and recognize that you are leaving a legacy.